SCRIPTURAL
CHRISTIANITY

Francis Asbury Publishing Company was founded in 1980 by several members of the Asbury community in Wilmore, Kentucky. Its aim was to meet the spiritual needs of that segment of the evangelical Christian public that is Wesleyan in outlook and to communicate the Wesleyan message to the larger Christian community.

In 1983 Francis Asbury Publishing Company became a part of Zondervan Publishing House. Its aim remains the spread of the Wesleyan message through the publication of popular, practical, and scholarly books for all Wesleyan denominations.

FRANCIS ASBURY PRESS
Box 7
Wilmore, Kentucky 40390

SCRIPTURAL CHRISTIANITY

A Call to
John Wesley's Disciples

Robert E. Chiles

FRANCIS ASBURY PRESS
of Zondervan Publishing House
1415 Lake Dr. S.E. • Grand Rapids, MI 49506

SCRIPTURAL CHRISTIANITY: A CALL TO JOHN WESLEY'S DISCIPLES
Copyright © 1984 by the Zondervan Corporation
Grand Rapids, Michigan

Francis Asbury Press is an imprint of Zondervan Publishing House
1415 Lake Drive, S.E., Grand Rapids, Michigan 49506

Library of Congress Cataloging in Publication Data
Chiles, Robert Eugene.
    Scriptural Christianity.

    Bibliography: p.
    Includes index.
    1. Wesley, John, 1703-1791. I. Title.
BX8495.W5C52   1984   230'.7   83-17024
ISBN 0-310-45781-5

Edited by Ben Chapman
Designed by Louise Bauer

Printed in the United States of America

83 84 85 86 87 88 — 10 9 8 7 6 5 4 3 2 1

CONTENTS

Preface   7

INTRODUCTION   11
  1 Backgrounds   13
  2 Bearers of Scriptural Christianity   21

PART ONE *The Journal:* The Acts of the Spirit   29
  3 The Work of God   33
  4 The Preaching of the Gospel   41
  5 The Offense of the Gospel   53
  6 The Community of the Spirit   65
  Another Journal Entry   79

PART TWO *The Letters:* Epistles of Apostolic Concern
                                                                 81
  7 The Call of John Wesley   85
  8 The Defense of the Gospel   95
  9 The Confirmation of the Gospel   107
  10 The Practice of Christianity   121
  A Letter to John Wesley   135

  Suggestions for Further Reading   137
  General Index   139

PREFACE

John Wesley and I are old friends. We became nodding acquaintances in the Methodist parsonage where I grew up. During my seminary days I studied his theology and our friendship ripened. In my doctoral study and subsequent writing he moved to the center of my work, and our friendship was confirmed. Though in recent years I have been occupied with other matters, we did not become estranged, but remained good friends who met only occasionally. This study has brought us together again, and it has been a pleasure to renew old interests and to discover that they have lost nothing of their fascination despite the passing years.

In this essay I have tried to let Wesley speak for himself. I have quoted liberally from his *Journal* and *Letters*, listed many additional references to them, and have not referred to the views of any other writer. The truth is that John Wesley doesn't need defenders or advocates for he has always been more than capable of fending for himself. I have tried to present the most substantial case possible for each of the themes I have lifted from his *Journal* and *Letters*. I have tried to be fair and to refrain from putting words into his mouth or slanting unduly the meaning he gives to the events he describes. I want the reader to decide if my presentations of Wesley's views are persuasive.

Perhaps I have oversimplified and neglected the context and historical developments of the issues and events I have recounted. The themes I have elected to develop seem important and germane to me. But I realize that other related and important themes have been slighted or omitted, and that other approaches to Wesley's writings are equally legitimate and may also be instructive.

I have a certain point of view from which I interpret Wesley. Basically, I locate him in the tradition of the Reformation—the continental Reformation as well as the English movement. I have tried, however, not to allow my stance to obtrude too frequently or blatantly. In a number of places, too, I have made assumptions and generalizations about points that remain in dispute among Wesley scholars who will easily detect them. By and large, I have thought it wise not to burden readers with the fine points of these debates. I believe that they will readily grasp Wesley's essential views, without the benefit of scholarly baggage and discussion. My biases and simplifications, I hope, will not seriously mislead anyone.

Some hints about what lies ahead. The historical survey in chapter 1 makes no pretense of doing justice to the vast and complicated subject it summarizes. Many readers will find little in it that is new. Chapter 2 introduces Wesley's *Journal* and *Letters* and addresses several procedural matters of interest to those who want to know why and how I chose to proceed as I have.

Part 1 (Chapters 3-6) suggests that Wesley's *Journal* is, in some ways, analogous to the Book of Acts. The *Journal* is also a record of the acts of the Spirit: manifested in the Wesleyan Revival; made effective through preaching; marked by resistance and opposition; and fulfilled in the Christian community.

Part 2 (Chapters 7-10) approaches Wesley's *Letters* as similar in many ways to St. Paul's letters in the New Testament. Wesley's *Letters* are, like Paul's, epistles of apostolic concern, written by a man called to maintain orthodoxy against opinion, reality against illusion, and faith active through works.

I have limited the sources for part 1 to the *Journal* and those in part 2 to the *Letters*. Obviously each of these sources might have been used to supplement the themes derived from the other. Treating them separately, however, gives the presentation sharper focus and makes fol-

8

low-up reading and research easier. Trying to say all that should be said on each issue, based only on one source or the other, has been a challenge. Whatever success I have achieved is a tribute to the abundance and consistency of these two Wesleyan writings.

At the conclusion of part 1, I have appended a journal entry of my own, and at the end of part 2, I included a letter to John Wesley. These are quite personal and may reveal as much about me as they do about Wesley. It seemed preferable to concentrate my private reflections and personal judgments in this manner rather than to scatter them throughout the text. I have tried not to get in Mr. Wesley's way.

Finally, in order to improve the flow of thought and make reading easier, I have taken two liberties. First, I have simplified the form used in introducing quotations, and, with two exceptions, have shown longer quotations as part of the text. Second, rather than consign references to a multitude of footnotes, I have inserted them into the text in abbreviated form. Within the parentheses the roman numeral identifies the volume and the arabic numeral the page of the reference cited in the *Journal* or the *Letters*.

Just how many references are enough to support a point that I contend Wesley makes "repeatedly," "many times," "again and again"? I may have listed too few rather than too many in my concern for readability. The reader who desires further confirmation is invited to consult Wesley's writings, which offer immediate assistance in their sizeable indexes. Nehemiah Curnock has provided an index (125 pp.) to the *Journal*, and John Telford a more modest (70 pp.) index to the *Letters*. Although their interests in these indexes differ somewhat from those I have pursued, the reader can find related passages through them easily and sometimes in quantity.

Bibliographical data for Curnock's edition of the *Journal* and Telford's edition of the *Letters* are given in the suggestions for further reading. I have also listed there a few books that may be of interest to the nontechnical reader.

This study had its inception some years ago in response to an invitation from Drew University to participate in the Tipple Lecture series by presenting some papers on Wesley's *Journal* and *Letters*. Part of what is here was first presented there.

I have accumulated a fair number of debts in my intermittent work on this project and am pleased now to express my gratitude to: Drew University for the invitation that started the project on its way; the Concord United Methodist Church for the freedom to pursue it; Jean Reiss and Jane Capstick for checking quotations and references; Kenneth Rowe for continuing assistance at the Drew University library; Doris and Bill Rickel for making me comfortable in France and supporting my endeavors; Renata von Stoephasius for subduing some of my wayward efforts in style and reasoning; and to Loretta Seidenfaden, Barbara Stash, and Irene Miller for turning messy manuscripts into typed copy.

Introduction

1
Backgrounds

Two hundred years have passed since the official beginning of American Methodism. We are heirs of a tradition but we are, as well, creatures of a day. History invites us to improve the time that is ours by making more explicit and effective our involvement in the tradition that is ours.

American Methodists and others interested in this branch of Protestant Christianity may wish to learn more about the persons and events identified with the beginning of the Wesleyan tradition. These pages are a modest contribution to that end. It is my purpose to sketch in them some basic features of the early Methodist movement, focusing on its head, John Wesley. These sketches are based on Wesley's published *Journal* and his collected *Letters*. I will say more in the next chapter about my reasons for selecting these particular sources.

In 1784, a relatively small band of Methodist preachers met in Baltimore for the so-called Christmas Conference, which resulted in the organization of Methodists in America as a separate church. Methodists had appeared in the new world earlier in the eighteenth century. Barbara Heck, Robert Strawbridge, and other lay persons brought their Methodist convictions with them to America and shared them with their friends and neighbors. A bit later, the first Methodist churches were organized. In New York City the John Street Church was established in 1766; in Philadelphia, St. George's Church was founded in 1767.

Since Wesley and British Methodism remained loyal to the crown during the events culminating in the Revolutionary War, American Methodists found themselves in an uneasy position. After independence was won, and at Wesley's direction, the American Methodist preachers met at the Christmas Conference and constituted American Methodism as a separate body, independent of legal ties to England and its established church, and free to develop as an indigenous church in the American context. They were, however, clearly bound by the doctrine and discipline that had come to define the Wesleyan societies in the mother country.

Freed from the suspicion of unpatriotic sentiments, American Methodism began to grow. It continued its unparalleled expansion for well over a century. In 1784, American Methodism numbered some 15,000 members in forty-six "circuits." A century later membership had increased to 2,700,000, and churches had multiplied.

The much heralded "circuit rider" was central to Methodism's phenomenal expansion. Circuit riders kept pace with the restless pioneers who spread across the Appalachian mountains, traversed the plains of the Midwest, and ventured into the Oregon territory in the far West. These hearty men literally lived in the saddle. Francis Asbury, the exemplar of these preachers and one of the first American bishops, is said to have traveled some 300,000 miles in the course of his duties.

Many of these itinerate preachers had in their charge organized Methodist groups in circuits spanning some five or six hundred miles. Regularly they traveled their circuits, pausing at appointed places to preach, baptize, marry, bury, and provide other pastoral services. After a few days they would move on to the next stop on their circuit. Every now and then they would visit new settlements, where they would organize churches of newly arrived Methodists and add the converts won by earnest preaching. Thus they followed the frontier westward.

Though not exclusively a Methodist institution, the camp meeting also promoted Methodist expansion. Held out of doors and lasting three or four days, these extended religious meetings drew isolated settlers from miles around. Preaching, prayer, and hymn singing dominated these meetings. Not only did they serve the social needs of hardworking people, far removed from one another, but they also met the settlers' religious need for a vital faith to sustain them in the rigors of frontier life.

The circuit rider and the camp meeting were but two of the more important "means of grace" employed by Wesley's Methodists in their conquest of the continent. They also maintained a number of Wesley's practices and devised still others to meet their particular needs. They cast their fortunes with those of a new country in a new world. Their religious allegiance, however, was fixed firmly across the ocean on the evangelical realities of the Wesleyan Revival.

In the course of its development in the nineteenth century, Methodism experienced divisions as did most denominations in America. Separate black churches were formed early in the century and grew rapidly after the Civil War. Out of concern for lay representation and fear of episcopal power, Methodist Protestantism declared its independence in 1830. Tensions arising from the struggle over slavery halved the Methodist Episcopal Church north and south roughly at the Mason-Dixon line in 1844. Smaller groups separated from the parent body: the Wesleyan Methodists in 1843, the Free Methodists in 1860.

Early in the twentieth century, movements toward separation gave way to movements toward reunification. In 1939 extended efforts brought together in one body the two branches of the Methodist Episcopal Church and the Methodist Protestant Church. This "new" Methodist Church accepted a black, segregated Central Jurisdiction that continued for nearly thirty years. In 1968 long-standing negotiations produced the United Methodist Church from the merger of the Methodist Church and the Evangelical United Brethren Church, a denomination derived from largely German-speaking churches that from their beginning had shared the Wesleyan heritage. About a dozen smaller Wesleyan-Methodist groups retain their denominational independence to the present time.

The 1982 *Yearbook of American and Canadian Church* reports 9,600,000 members in the United Methodist Church gathered in some 36,000 churches. Methodism has become the second-largest Protestant denomination in America, exceeded in size only by the Southern Baptist Convention with more than thirteen million members. The full "family" of American Methodism, composed of all its related denominations, has thirteen million members—somewhat less than the family of Baptist denominations, which has sixteen million members. Worldwide, Methodism has eighteen million adherents.

Briefly, this is the story of Methodism in America. But this story began in England and, to make it complete, we must move back in time to the revival that takes its name from John Wesley.

Perhaps we should begin by noting that the Wesleyan Revival was part of a broader movement of religious renewal that gained prominence in several countries in the early eighteenth century. In 1734 the preaching of Jonathan Edwards was attended by "a very remarkable blessing" that spread throughout New England and along the Atlantic seaboard. This work was assisted by George Whitefield, an early associate of Wesley, whose preaching occasioned great response on his several extensive tours of America. In Germany also evangelical zeal found new expressions and successes among the Moravians. Calvinist groups in Scotland and Wales had already begun to experience renewed vitality and effectiveness before Wesley's evangelical breakthrough. The Good News spread. Each of these groups learned about the manifestations of God's power elsewhere and was thus encouraged in its own efforts. It seemed that the world was astir under the prompting of a benevolent providence, and many laborers went forth to reap the burgeoning harvest.

It is not necessary to argue for Methodism's primacy or uniqueness in this general religious awakening. It may be said, however, that the Wesleyan Revival was distinguished by some of its emphases and innovations: its field preaching and use of lay preachers; its intimate group life in societies, classes, bands, and love feasts; its con-

ferences, connectional system, and educational efforts;
and its universal evangelical appeal and fervent hymn
singing.

It may be noted, further, that the Wesleyan Revival
was blessed with singular leadership. Wesley was distinguished by his apostolic zeal in preaching the gospel; his
skill in gathering and nurturing religious societies; the
length of his uninterrupted service; and by his writings,
which were unusually voluminous and broad in scope.

John Wesley was born in 1703 in Epworth, Lincolnshire, to the Anglican clergyman Samuel Wesley and his
wife Susanna. John was the fifteenth and his brother
Charles the eighteenth in the family of nineteen children.
Susanna Wesley provided each child with a stern but
sound education. John attended Oxford University, was
ordained deacon in the Church of England in 1725, elected
a fellow of Lincoln College in 1726, and ordained a priest
in 1728.

Wesley's England was in particular need of religious
awakening. Religion and morality were at low ebb.
Though the form of religion was evident, its power was
largely lacking. For many in the "better classes," manners
seemed more important than morals. Poorly attended religious services were often dry, routine, and unedifying.
Clergy frequently were more occupied with worldly matters than with affairs of the spirit. Wesley was appalled
at the laxity of the clergy, the impotence of the church,
and the malaise that afflicted its members. He was also
much concerned for his own spiritual estate. If England
needed to be awakened, so did he.

While still a tutor at Oxford University in 1729, he
began meeting with his brother Charles and others who
shared his concerns. The members of this "Holy Club"
convened regularly to read the Scriptures, to examine the
state of their faith, to encourage one another in spiritual
growth, and to devise measures for Christian service. In
1735, Wesley joined William Oglethorpe's expedition to

the English colony in Georgia, where for two years he applied himself to his religious duties with unabated vigor. His efforts were largely ineffective, however, and he was more distressed than heartened by this experience. Returning to England, Wesley continued his pursuit of inner peace and a sustaining hold on the gospel. At length his restless spirit found what it had sought for so long. On May 24, 1738, at Aldersgate Street in London, at the meeting of a small religious society and while listening to Luther's preface to the Book of Romans, Wesley felt his "heart strangely warmed." Strong in the faith that had finally grasped him, he put aside his endless self-examination, his consuming doubts, and his fear of failure. He became a dauntless herald of the good news that, apart from our striving, God accepts us as we are and strengthens us in faith to become His sons and loyal servants. The Wesleyan Revival was under way.

In the following fifty years Wesley is said to have preached 40,000 sermons and traveled 250,000 miles in his service to God. He died in 1791 at the age of eighty-eight, active to the very end in his ardent apostleship in the Revival.

The different aspects of the life and development of the Revival, the realities that made it effective, and the role that Wesley played in it make up the story that unfolds in the following pages.

The Revival affected Britain as well as America and much of the English-speaking world. It had an impact also on many German-speaking people in America through the work of Philip William Otterbein, Jacob Albright, and others touched by the Wesleyan spirit. Now worldwide, Methodism has become a large, significant, and committed branch of Protestant Christianity and a full participant in the wider ecumenical movements of the twentieth century. American Methodism, involving some thirteen million members, is an eloquent testimony to the Revival's success.

2
Bearers of Scriptural Christianity

L ittle guesswork is needed to reconstruct the history of the Wesleyan Revival and Wesley's role in it. From his own hand we possess a veritable flood of material. The question we face is which of his many sources to use and, above all, how to use them.

This chapter offers an answer to this question and fixes the direction for the remainder of our discussion. It contains my reasons for choosing Wesley's *Journal* and *Letters* from among his many writings, my contention that these sources are bearers of scriptural Christianity, and my attempt to interpret them against the background of the Book of Acts and Paul's epistles. In that way our task becomes manageable; as a further benefit, some readers may even be led to read the original sources themselves.

Wesley's pen was prodigiously productive. His writings fill more than thirty volumes in the editions in common use. They may be grouped in the following manner: His primary *Sermons* comprise two volumes; he designated them as "standards" for Methodist doctrine and discipline, together with his *Explanatory Notes on the New Testament*. This volume contains a revised translation of the biblical text and a commentary. His additional sermons, minutes, polemical, and miscellaneous writings claim approximately five volumes in the comprehensive edition of his *Works*. His published *Journal* is a set of eight large volumes, and his collected *Letters* fill yet another set of that size. If we include his efforts in hymnody and poetry with those of his brother Charles, we add another thirteen volumes to the total. A new, definitive edition of Wesley's works is now being issued; it will comprise thirty-four sizeable volumes.

All of these writings are important for a critical understanding of Wesley and the early Methodist movement. Our purpose here, however, is much less ambitious. By concentrating only on part of this vast literature, we gain more immediate access to and attain a sharper focus on this formative period in Methodist history. Consequently, I have confined myself to Wesley's *Journal* and *Letters* and based my account on these two publications.

These two sources are particularly appropriate and useful for several reasons. They afford us first-hand contact with the people and events of the Revival. They tend to be direct, immediate, and a true reflection of the human situation. They are sometimes intimate and often revealing of character and action. They transport us through space and time and involve us personally in the Revival.

Furthermore, putting these two sources front and center may enliven our regard for these neglected literary forms. Journal keeping was a common practice in Wesley's time. A great number of persons, both great and small, kept journals. Many were convinced that God's purpose for their lives could thus be better discerned among the welter of their daily affairs. Letter writing was also a major occupation of the age. An indispensable form of communication, correspondence was taken seriously and practiced widely. Letters were written more frequently then and more thoughtfully and skillfully than now. Journal keeping and letter writing required time, thought, and commitment. Both forms of communication benefited both those who wrote and those who read.

Finally, our study can serve as an introduction to these two imposing collections of Wesley's writings. Their magnitude and detail are sufficient to give pause to the most intrepid interpreter. To the person of casual interest, they may well seem insurmountable. Combined, the *Journal* and *Letters* total sixteen volumes and 7,000 pages; enough, it would seem, to support the modest purpose of this undertaking. In fact, these selected sources must themselves be treated selectively, if our purpose is not to be defeated. More about this later.

The dimensions of our task can be specified more concretely by describing the general characteristics of these

23

writings. Wesley's *Journal* is an awesome achievement even for an age in which journal keeping was the thing to do. In 1739 Wesley began to publish extracts from his more extensive personal journey. In all, twenty-one such extracts or parts were put into print during his lifetime. Early in this century, Nehemiah Curnock placed Methodism under debt by publishing the definitive edition of the *Journal*. This standard edition consumes more than 4,000 pages and fills eight volumes. It contains thousands of entries, often recorded day by day, extending from 1735 to 1790. Curnock amplified the *Journal* text with transcriptions from various of Wesley's private diaries whose shorthand and code he laboriously deciphered. He added a multitude of notes supplying context and historical details indispensable for the understanding of many entries and issues. The story of this edition as told in the first volume is as fascinating as a good detective story.

The *Journal* is not only big, it is also diverse and far ranging. Little seems to have been excluded. It tells of Wesley's trip to Georgia and his struggle toward Aldersgate. It refers repeatedly to his preaching, its arrangements and problems, its successes and failures. It takes us on the travels of an inexhaustible itinerant—throughout England, to Ireland, Scotland, and the continent. It contains his shrewd observations about congregations and mobs, priests and princes, and rich and poor. It informs us about his wide-ranging scholarship and his pursuit of knowledge in many fields. It illustrates his interests in medicine, health, the supernatural, science, literature, theatre, politics, economics, and social welfare. It exhibits variety almost without end.

Wesley's journal keeping and other activities seem not to have hampered yet another exercise of his pen: letter writing. Many of his letters were called forth by the duties of his apostleship as he proposed initiatives or made responses to his correspondents; many were personal or otherwise incidental to the life of the Revival. It seems that a number have been lost. Those that remain, however, represent more than sixty years of Wesley's ministry and provide us with ample material for study.

John Telford edited the now standard eight-volume collection of Wesley's *Letters* in 1931. It contains 2,670 entries derived from many sources to supplement the mere 900 Thomas Jackson included in his third edition of Wesley's *Works* in 1831. Letters of this busy correspondent continue to turn up and one day will be included in an expanded collection. In his edition, Telford provides an introduction to each letter, supplying us with biographical details, historical background, and interpretative insights.

Wesley's *Letters* display an enormous variety. They address all sorts of persons, subjects, and situations. They vary dramatically in length. They tantalize with a terse one-line note to an embattled preacher: "John White, whoever is wrong, you are not right" (VII, 227), and they have room for a seventy-six-page dissertation addressed to Dr. Conyers Middleton, refuting his charges of enthusiasm among the Methodists (II, 312 ff.). They include an extensive controversial correspondence, along with often aroused responses to editors of various publications. They deal in substantial numbers with organizational and connectional matters. They offer spiritual counsel, affirm friendship, disclose self-examination, make confession, voice satisfaction, express gratitude, and pronounce benediction. They reveal the encompassing concerns of a full life.

In restricting our study to the *Journal* and the *Letters*, we have limited our field somewhat. Though we have not settled all our procedural problems, we have come to the heart of the matter. In themselves, our selected sources are pretty formidable as we have just noted. We need therefore to narrow our focus still more.

Now and again Wesley identified himself as "a man

of one book." That book, of course, was the Bible, and he was content to be known as a "Bible bigot." Often, too, he described Methodism as a deliberate rendition of "Scriptural Christianity." Fidelity to Scripture as it comes alive in evangelical experience was his first and last concern. Perhaps, then, we will not go far wrong if we use scriptural Christianity as the key to our interpretation of the *Journal* and *Letters*.

More specifically, I propose to interpret the *Journal* against the background of the Book of Acts and the suggestion that although there are obvious differences both are intimate first-hand records of the work of the Spirit through dedicated men of God. In similar fashion, I propose to interpret the *Letters* with reference to the epistles of St. Paul and to suggest that in their correspondence both Paul and John Wesley address their duties in strikingly similar ways.

There are other options. We might argue that, despite its great variety, the *Journal* exhibits a unity that is derived from its author's "unreserved consecration to one task." Much can be said for this view, but this unity in variety can also be accounted for in another way. We can ascribe it to the work of the Holy Spirit that underlies and reaches out through Wesley's "unreserved consecration." Thus, in my interpretation of the *Journal*, I place more emphasis on the activity of the Spirit in initiating and supporting Wesley's work than I do on Wesley's response to the leading of the Spirit.

Again, we might look at the *Letters* as a restatement of Paul's theology to which seeking Christians have returned age after age to renew their faith and to fuel the fires of revival and reformation. And much can also be said for this view. Taking a somewhat different tack, I regard the *Letters* as epistles of Christian concern, as expressions of Wesley's passion to defend and confirm the faith following its bestowal by the Spirit. If the stress in the *Journal* may be said to fall on divine grace as it works among men and women, the stress in the *Letters* may be said to fall on the responsibility for conserving and extending this gracious work. If the *Journal* records the work of God in the Revival, the *Letters* reflect Wesley's sensitivity and devotion to the furtherance of that work.

The Book of Acts and the Pauline correspondence provide rich interpretative backgrounds. I will attempt to state in broad and general terms some implications of these New Testament writings for our examination of Wesley's *Journal* and *Letters*. For the most part, the evident parallels between New Testament and Wesleyan writings will provide the outline for my interpretations.

Of course, to assume too close a connection between these writings may be misleading. Yet it is not necessary to canonize Wesley's writings to contend for important parallels between them and their suggested counterparts in the New Testament. I suspect that there are additional correlations between these literatures, and while they will not be examined here, they may well merit further exploration.

To be sure, Wesley's writings are closely related not only to the Book of Acts and the letters of Paul but also to the synoptic Gospels and particularly to the Johannine literature. Some of Wesley's most dearly loved expressions of Christianity are found in these last-named sources. Still, because of their character and their role in the Revival, the *Journal* and *Letters* seem most closely linked to Acts and Paul. Whatever the objections may be to relating Wesley's writings to the New Testament in this fashion, our basic contention is secure. "Primitive" Methodism recognized but one standard: scriptural Christianity!

Part One

THE JOURNAL
The Acts of
the Spirit

"You shall receive power when the Holy Spirit has come upon you; and you shall be my witnesses in Jerusalem, and in all Judea and Samaria and to the end of the earth."

Acts 1:8 (RSV)

John Wesley's *Journal* has often been regarded as striking proof of the continuing creativity of the Spirit of God that animated the New Testament Church. His *Journal* entries portrayed the dramatic conquest of the souls by the Holy Spirit in ways similar to those recorded in the Book of Acts.

Very simply, we can draw several significant parallels between the *Journal* and Acts. Both inform the world about striking occurrences that refer beyond themselves to divine reality. Both record the work of God as alive and creative, filling those it touches with a sense of urgent expectancy. Both contain action-packed stories of venturing faith and mighty deeds. Both describe events that bear witness to the Good News that God refuses to be excused from human affairs and that he persistently insinuates Himself into their midst. Perhaps the conclusion is too obvious to bear repetition: the acts of true servants of God are acts of God's Spirit whether done in the first, the eighteenth, or the twentieth century.

With this understanding, Wesley's *Journal* is an account of a man and a movement transparent to God. It informs us about biography and history, and, perhaps more important, it informs us about God and His ways. The acts it records are acts of an apostle to those in need, and they will be understood as acts begun, continued, and ended in the power of the Spirit.

In these pages, much will have to remain unsaid about the character and life of Wesley, his Christian experience, and his theological understanding. I will seek to picture Wesley in the light of his understanding of the significance of his work. Unswervingly, he ascribed his "accomplishments" to divine grace. (1) The Revival, he said, is the work of God. (2) Preaching is effective only as God inspires and elicits response to it. (3) The offense that the gospel arouses depicts the struggle between God and the power of sin. (4) The community of the Spirit is called into being and continued in power by God's action through the Holy Spirit. These are four ways in which Wesley acknowledged divine initiative; a detailed discussion of these themes is contained in the chapters that follow in part 1.

Nearly every page in the *Journal* convinces the reader of the graciousness of God. The dramatic acts it records impress many as vivid proof of what God can do with a human life. The *Journal* reminds the faithful that this record has not been completed, and that further chapters are yet to be added to this story of God's activity through modern-day apostles.

3
The Work of God

Pentecost and Aldersgate appear side by side on the church calendar of Methodism. Though coincidental, this fact is instructive. In the Book of Acts, Pentecost is interpreted as the coming of the Holy Spirit to followers of the Christ and as the birth of the church. Aldersgate commonly is interpreted as the coming of the Spirit to John Wesley and, in one sense, as the "birth" of the Methodist movement. Both accounts describe the Spirit's work in releasing two men from uncertainty, awakening them to a presence, and endowing them with power. The invasion of the Spirit was the prelude to intensive activity that spread the gospel from place to place to the ends of the earth.

Wesley was aware of the parallels between the events in Acts and those he characterized in the course of the Revival. Repeatedly he referred to Acts, expounded its relevant passages, and appealed to it as he sought to grasp and interpret the meaning of the Revival (II, 65, 386-89; III, 51). Perhaps it is not too much to say that the *Journal* grew out of and served the early Methodist movement in somewhat the same way that Acts grew out of and served the early church. Both witness to the power of the Holy Spirit in these great awakenings as it created, guided, and extended the life of these movements.

Wesley consciously treated part III of the *Journal,* which dates from September 17, 1738, to November 1, 1739, as the specific documentation of a great work that God had begun among His people (II, 67-305). That work continued, and at the end of his ministry he looked back more than fifty years to "what God has wrought since that time" (VIII, 38). The phrase, "the work of God" is one of the most familiar in the *Journal.* This phrase or its equivalent is repeated constantly as Wesley considered the divine activity in which he shared. To explain and justify the movement "vulgarly called Methodist," he often gave accounts of these works. These accounts were his vivid testimony to God's goodness and power and His purpose to save His people (VII, 108).

But let us raise another issue before we elaborate this theme. History suggests that few leaders of religious revival claim credit for the successes of their movements. Invariably they attribute their triumphs to the effective power of God. Is it legitimate, therefore, to inquire if this is what they really believed in their heart of hearts? Might not the actions of some would-be apostles indicate that under their breath they qualify their declaration of obeisance: "God is at work, to be sure. But I have labored valiantly also. Without my efforts God would have been hard-pressed to produce these impressive results." We need to search Wesley's words and actions to try to determine if they are consistent, and if he really meant it when he asserted that the Revival was the "work of God." Pride can be veiled by humility, and it is not always easy to separate the two.

Several factors need to be explored in our effort to answer this question of integrity: (1) Wesley's constant assignment of the Revival's sweeping power and magnitude to "the work of God"; (2) his reliance on providential openings in the ordering of his own activities; (3) his appeal to the fruits of the Spirit as the sure test of the validity of the Revival; and (4) his attribution of religious decline to human causes.

It is doubtful whether Wesley considered the Revival the product of his planning or activity any more than Peter and Paul considered the New Testament church their creation. He proclaimed that the work is wholly dependent on God, and though we falter and fail, God in His goodness, in His own time, can majestically succeed. As Wesley inquires, "Why should we despair of seeing good done in any place? How soon can God turn the wilderness into a fruitful field" (V, 196)! And again, "It seems God was pleased to pour out His Spirit this year on every part, both of England and Ireland, perhaps in a manner we have never seen before, certainly not for twenty years" (IV, 477). And yet again, "About noon I preached at Oxford. I have seen no such prospect here for many years. The congregation was large and still as night, although many gentlemen were among them. The next evening the house would not contain the congregation; yet all were quiet, even those that could not come in. And I believe God not only opened their understandings, but began a good work in some of their hearts" (VI, 375).

In the spread of the Revival and its effects on the lives of many, Wesley found a sure sign that God was at work. He observed the marvelous changes that occurred in Dublin and in London, in Oxford and Epworth and was moved to remark how mightily God had wrought (IV, 519; VI, 299, 352-53). Those who had been converted attested to a new reality in which they shared. And in these places, as well as in a host of others, an evident transformation of manners and morals pointed to the grace of God. "I preached at Bradford," he writes, "where the people are all alive. Many here have lately experienced the great salvation, and their zeal has been a general blessing. Indeed, this I always observe—wherever a work of sanctification breaks out the whole work of God prospers" (VI, 73). Exhibiting his pastoral concern, he records this experience: "I began what I had long intended, visiting the society from house to house, setting apart at least two hours in a day for that purpose. I was surprised to find the simplicity with which one and all spoke, both of their temporal and spiritual state. Nor could I have easily have known, by any other means, how great a work God has wrought among them. I found exceedingly little to reprove, but much to praise God for" (VI, 126-27).

Wesley was well informed about similar transformations that were taking place among people in New England, Germany, and throughout much of the world. He delighted in reading accounts of God's work in these distant places to the evening meetings of his societies to impress on them the magnitude of what God was doing (II, 84; III, 122, 331, 449; IV, 54). Part XIX of the *Journal* is pervaded by deep rejoicing over the work that is prospering (VI, 249-367). And in Wesley's judgment it was God's work. So overwhelmed was he that he described it in ecstatic terms. It is "amazing," "marvelous," "wonderous," "glorious" (IV, 122, 387; V, 17; VIII, 46). For him the Revival was a new creation, an unexpected, unplanned bounty from God's hand.

Often Wesley thought about taking advantage of God's providential openings as they became manifest. The *Journal* contains comparatively little long-range planning and few carefully calculated strategies. Rather, its entries embody the daring and deceptively simple tactic of following where God leads. Wesley was content to let God be God and to follow after, trusting the harvest to Him. He makes this humbling acknowledgment: "How plain an evidence have we here that even our outward work, even the societies, are not of man's building! With all our labour and skill, we cannot, in nine years' time, form a society in this place" (IV, 27). And in the same vein, about a community where he had had little success: "Will God revive His work even in this sink of wickedness, and after so many deadly stumbling-blocks?" (VI, 192). Such entries are legion. Human design and determination seem not to be ultimate; it is God's good pleasure to will and to do. Prayerfully and earnestly, Wesley strove to find the "openings" provided by God. Then, however unexpected or unbecoming, however unsophisticated or unorthodox the demands, he employed such means and "innovations" as might be required to bring them before the redeeming power of God.

God's providence so ordered the world, Wesley believed, that things happen at the "right time." His responsibility was not to arrange such times but only in faith to discern them and to give himself to them (VIII,

10). After considering in conference the possibility of sending a missionary to the East Indies, he writes, "after the matter had been fully considered, we were unanimous in our judgment that we have no call thither yet, no invitation, no providential opening of any kind" (VI, 476). On one of his journeys by ship, ill winds forced him to land before he had intended to. "I found we had still a little society here," he records. "I had not seen them for thirteen years, and had no thought of seeing them now; but God does all things well. In the evening I preached" (VII, 311, 320). He seemed to have been aware of the dangers in relying so fully on insight into God's providence—but aware, too, of the dangers of inaction. Again and again he accepted the risks attending his conviction that there are times and circumstances in which God does "make bare his arm," and others in which He does not (I, 429).

Wesley granted the difficulty in intuiting God's intention in revival. But he also believed that the fruits of revival mark it indelibly as the work of God. On the title page of the third part of the *Journal,* he quotes Acts 5:38-39: "If this counsel or this work be of men, it will come to nought; but if it be of God, ye cannot overthrow it; lest haply ye be found even to fight against God" (II, 65). Wesley indicates that it is his purpose in this extract "to declare to all mankind what it is that the Methodists (so-called) have done, and are doing now—or, rather, what it is that God hath done, and is still doing, in our land. For it is not the work of man which hath lately appeared. All who calmly observe it must say, 'This is the Lord's doing, and it is marvellous in our eyes'" (II, 67). The test of the Revival, he contended, was to be found in its results; they resist all wordly explanation. Repeatedly he made this appeal.

Wesley did not propose to hold God responsible, however, if people failed to respond or fell from grace. The advances of the Revival he attributed to God, but its decline he attributed to God's creatures. If they were unconcerned, or if they fell away, they, not God, must bear the burden of failure. Wesley knew that the first flush of power in revival often failed to last, and that many of its fine flowers would not bear fruit. "Abundance of blossoms," he sighs of those in one responsive group, "but when the sun is up, how many of these will wither away" (V, 345)! He seems to possess an honest realism that will surprise those who regard him as an ardent perfectionist. An unexpected increase in a society moves him to comment, "such a shower of grace never continued long; and afterwards men might resist the Holy Ghost as before. When the general ferment subsides, every one that partook of it has his trial for life; and the higher the flood, the lower will be the ebb; yea, the more swiftly it rose, the more swiftly it falls. So that, if we see this here, we should not be discouraged. We should only use all diligence to encourage as many as possible to press forward in spite of all the refluent tide" (VII, 67).

In a number of places he analyzed the causes of the decay of the vast work of God and pointed to factors such as these: people mistakenly become wise in their own eyes; they become bigots in opinions and worship; they seldom teach and little practice self-denial (IV, 123; VI, 25). Again, because of the rise and decline of curiosity attending the Revival, and because of the hope and the inevitable offense that the gospel arouses, "the number of hearers in every place may be expected first to increase, and then decrease" (IV, 175). The decline in the work of God was further hastened if it was taken for granted. Thus Wesley writes, "how does the frequency and greatness of the works of God make us less (instead of more) sensible of them! A few years ago, if we heard of one notorious sinner truly converted to God, it was a matter of solemn joy to all that loved or feared Him: and now that multitudes of every kind and degree are daily turned from the power of darkness to God, we pass it over as a common thing! O, God, give us thankful hearts" (III, 400).

How persuasive is Wesley's contention that it is divine grace that initiates and sustains the work of God? Little negative evidence has been cited, chiefly because little is to be found in the *Journal*. Also, as noted in the preface, it is my intention to present Wesley's case in the most favorable terms. These qualifications notwithstanding, we acknowledge that in countless instances his words consistently support his claim that the Revival was the work of God. Through fifty years of unceasing service, his actions, too, seem amply to uphold his conviction. Nor do we find evidence of any disjunction between his words and his actions. His unexpressed thought and unconscious motivation, however, are nearly impossible to ascertain. What hints we can pick up seem to confirm, not to confound, his assertion of the priority of grace. In other words, all available evidence seems to support the sincerity of Wesley's claim. His actions and his words sustain his conviction that the Revival is the work of God and not man. What he thought and felt in the inner recesses of his being remains hidden in the counsels of an all-knowing providence.

This then is the first point to be made about the acts of the Spirit working through John Wesley. The task in which he is engaged is the work of God to whom he is unfeignedly thankful. It is no pious pretense that impels him to affirm that all is of grace—rather, it is part and parcel of his thought, his work, and his life.

40

4
The Preaching of the Gospel

The Book of Acts and Wesley's *Journal* are chronicles filled with accounts of preaching. To test this proposition, try deleting from either the preaching of the Word; the journeys made in order to preach; the efforts to gather congregations and secure preaching places; the enthusiastic response, hostile rejection, or stolid unconcern of listeners; and the pastoral oversight of those who are won through preaching. The remainder would make little sense.

Both records show apostles eager to tell the good news of how God in Christ had set them free and committed them to preach the gospel to all who had need. Both records depict the evangelistic mission of the church; filled with dramatic scenes and heroic actions, they are arresting in their reports of bold successes, often in the face of bitter resistance. When God's Spirit has free course in human life, such things are not unusual. According to these two sources, the principal instrument through which the Spirit moved was the preaching of the Word, in season and out—the good word of what God had done on behalf of His people.

My purpose here is not so much to observe *how* Wesley preached or *what* he said as to portray the role of his preaching in the Revival and to report his estimation of its significance and power. We will see that he relied on the Spirit to guide and assist his preaching and to elicit response from his listeners. The apostle preaches, but it is God who brings forth the harvest. The role that preaching played in the Revival is another basic theme in the *Journal* that marks it as a record of the acts of the Spirit.

Preaching was indeed central to the Wesleyan Revival, an assertion that is well supported in Wesley's *Journal.* Evidence of this abounds, but before we look at it several important and related questions should be raised: Why do some preachers evoke an overwhelming response while others encounter indifference or rejection?

What can a preacher do to enhance the effectiveness of his sermons? Is there any relationship between the kind of gospel a preacher presents and the sort of response he receives? Is preaching an exercise in aggression, or even coercion, covered by avowals of selfless service? Is it an opportunity for the preacher to attack defenseless listeners and vent his hostility on them? Is it an invitation to egoistic self-elevation?

Perhaps the basic issue inherent in all these questions is this: Is preaching an audacious, demanding undertaking, essentially dependent on consecrated human effort, or is it an undertaking dependent for its authenticity and efficacy on divine grace?

To try to ascertain Wesley's answer to this basic question and to illuminate some of the others we have raised, we will examine several aspects of his preaching and its role in the Revival as reflected in the *Journal*. The following points seem to be significant: (1) Wesley's insistence that the preacher assume the responsibilities proper to his task; (2) his conviction that preaching is made effective through the operation of the Holy Spirit; (3) his testimony to the assistance of the Spirit in his own preaching; and (4) his certainty that ultimately the response of his hearers, whether favorable or unfavorable, rests in God's hands. In brief, Wesley seems fully persuaded that even though the preacher has responsibilities, he does not control the outcome of his preaching—God does.

The first responsibility of the preacher is to proclaim the gospel, which is the heart of scriptural Christianity. In this insistence Wesley was unswerving throughout his work in the Revival. In 1740, referring to his Aldersgate experience, he writes, "two years ago it pleased God to show us the *old way* of salvation by *faith only*" (II, 354). Much later he notes, "I strongly enforced the first principles (which indeed never can be too much enforced), 'By grace are ye saved through faith' " (VII, 327-28). A bit later he observes that he applied "once more what I had enforced fifty years before, 'By grace are ye saved through faith' " (VII, 357).

Now and then Wesley was accused of recommending salvation through good works. But he regularly disavowed these charges and admits that he comes "within a hair's breadth of Calvinism" and its denial of human agency. He rarely wavers on this point: "I was desired to preach that evening on 'Work out your own salvation with fear and trembling; for it is God that worketh in you both to will and to do of His good pleasure.' Even the Calvinists," he exults, "were satisfied for the present, and readily acknowledged that we did not ascribe our salvation to our own works, but to the grace of God" (VI, 304). In his *Journal* he included a letter to the editor of *Lloyd's Evening Post*, refuting several charges. In his rebuttal he asserts, "but the Methodists do not hold 'good works meritorious.' No; neither does ours or any other Protestant Church" (IV, 419).

Clearly, faith is the desired consequence of preaching. Men must cease to trust themselves before they can begin to trust God. In Wesley's words: "I endeavoured to cut them off from all false supports and vain dependencies by explaining and applying that fundamental truth, 'To him that worketh not, but believeth on Him that justifieth the ungodly, his faith is counted for righteousness' " (II, 294).

Persuaded that the "old way" alone had the power of salvation, he deplored preaching that failed to present the gospel in its fullness. "I brought strange things to the ears of those that had been used to softer doctrines," he asserts, "and I believe not in vain" (VI, 309). On another occasion he reports, "I heard a sermon setting forth the *duty* of *getting a good estate* and *keeping a good reputation*. It is possible to deny (supposing the Bible to be true) that such a preacher is a 'blind leader of the blind' " (II, 377)? Preaching may fail also if it does not make the sermon's implications plain to its listeners: "This very day I heard many excellent truths delivered in the kirk; but, as there was no application, it was likely to do as much good as the singing of a lark . . . no sinners are convinced of sin, none converted to God, by this way of preaching" (VI, 239).

Wesley was consistently rigorous in the application of his standards of authentic preaching. He scornfully compares true and false preaching: "One who was a believer falls into carelessness or willful sin. If he comes to hear our preaching, then we shake all his bones in pieces. If he comes to them, they stroke him and lull him to sleep. Oh how does any backslider escape this comfortable preaching" (III, 154; II, 321)? Some sermons satisfy Wesley: "Oh how gracious is God to the poor sinners of St. Agnes! In the church and out of the church they hear the same great truths of the wrath of God against sin, and His love to those that are in Christ Jesus" (IV, 234). The preacher is to proclaim the gospel of salvation by grace through faith. Wesley seems prepared to settle for nothing less.

It should not be thought, however, that Wesley wanted preaching to be all condemnation and demand. God's mercy and love must be preached as well as His righteousness and justice. Wesley exonerates a society that had manifested only meager response because of the nature of the preaching its members had heard: "The people have been told, frequently and strongly, of their coldness, deadness, heaviness and littleness of faith, but rarely of anything that would move thankfulness. Hereby many were driven away and those that remained were kept cold and dead" (V, 225). Wesley believed that the offer of Christ was meaningful when sinners were encouraged to hope and were helped to reach out beyond their despair.

The preacher was also responsible for making the gospel relevant. He must assist the Spirit as much as he can. He must preach to reach the minds and meet the needs of his hearers and not "overshoot" his congregation (VIII, 55). Wesley was sensitive to the need to make the gospel relevant. On one occasion he notes that many of his congregation "were gay, genteel people: so I spake on the first elements of the gospel. But I was still out of their depth. Oh how hard it is to be shallow enough for a polite audience" (V, 429)!

As he labored with a group of backsliders, "a large company of quality" appeared. "I knew this was heathen Greek to them," he admits, "but I could not then change my subject. However, I diluted my discourse as much as I could, that it might not be quite too strong for their digestion" (V, 326). A short time later, distressed over a previous failure, he writes, "resolving not to shoot over their heads, as I had done the day before, I spoke strongly of death and judgement, heaven and hell," and, he says with satisfaction, "this they seemed to comprehend" (V, 455). In yet another difficult situation he decided to preach on the form and power of godliness. This subject, he concludes, "I judged to be far more suitable to such a congregation than talking of justification by faith" (VII, 126).

A preacher had additional responsibilities in spreading the gospel. Wesley took a first momentous step in 1739 when, encouraged by George Whitefield, he began field preaching. "I submitted to be more vile, and proclaimed in the highways the glad tidings of salvation" (II, 172). Later, reflecting on the propriety of field preaching, he writes that—compared with the indecency of St. Paul's, with people sleeping and talking during the service—field preaching was all dignity and propriety, the people behaving in a manner fitting to those who hear God (III, 373). Denied the use of the church at Epworth, he preached from his father's stone in the cemetery and did more good, he believed, than he had in several years' preaching inside the church (III, 19). He once went to examine a yard that had been suggested for a preaching service. "One circumstance of this I did not like," he protests. "It was plentifully furnished with stones—artillery ready at hand for the devil's drunken companions" (IV, 22). The following incident shows the kind of effort Wesley made to contact a needy soul. Traveling by horseback he encountered another rider and conversed with him. He concludes this entry, "being the better mounted of the two, I kept close to his side, and endeavoured to show him his heart" (III, 10).

But once the preacher has done all that he can to make preaching effective, it is only as preaching is caught up by the Spirit that it bears fruit. Wesley believed that the Spirit often used peculiar measures to arrange the preaching situation to make it effective: "How wisely does God order all things! Some will not hear even the word of God out of a church; for the sakes of these we are often permitted to preach in a church. Others will not hear it in a church; for their sakes we are often compelled to preach in the highways" (III, 290). Wesley was both surprised and satisfied that God was able to make all things work out for the best. A clergyman once offered Wesley his church for morning preaching, but the key to the church could not be found. "So I made a virtue of necessity," says Wesley, "and preached near the Cross Street; probably to double the congregation which would have been in the church" (VI, 453).

During the more violent demonstrations, mobs frequently threw stones at Wesley. But in this terse observation he confirms that God rules even in such a circumstance: "One man was bawling just at my ear when a stone struck him on the cheek, and he was still" (III, 373; II, 283). In several places he concedes casually that the prospect of trouble or danger increased the size of his congregation. He seemed quite willing to accept this increase in numbers as a mark of God's grace (II, 208, 212).

As Wesley sees it, God often utilized quite extraordinary means to effect his ends: "High and low, rich and poor, now flocked together from all quarters; and all were eager to hear, except one man, who was the town crier. He began to bawl amain, till his wife ran to him and literally stopped the noise: she seized him with one hand and clapped the other upon his mouth, so that he could not get out one word. God then began a work which I am persuaded will not soon come to an end" (VI, 526). He sets down a parallel incident: "One big man, exceeding drunk, was very noisy and turbulent, till his wife . . . seized him by the collar, gave him two or three hearty boxes on the ear, and dragged him away like a calf. But at length he got out of her hands, crept in among the people and stood quiet as a lamb" (VI, 284). It seems that God is pleased now and then to use strong and faithful women to further His cause!

Wesley also pointed to the particular assistance of the Spirit he himself received in his preaching. "It pleased God to give me uncommon liberty," he testifies frequently (VII, 31, 68; VII, 435). "I spoke with such closeness and pungency as I cannot do but at some peculiar seasons. It is indeed the gift of God, and cannot be attained by all the efforts of nature and art united" (V, 414). He acknowledged that it was the Spirit that led him to speak beyond the accustomed time, to overcome illness, and to be heard at the edge of large congregations (V, 373, 378, 524). "Feeling myself much as I was eleven years ago, and now knowing how short my time of working might be, I resolved to do a little while I could. So I began at five; and though I scarce could be heard at first, yet the more I spoke the more my voice was strengthened. Before I had half done, everyone could hear. To God be all the glory" (VII, 83). And again he writes, "I have now preached thrice a day for seven days following; but it is just the same as if it had been but one" (VI, 324). And yet again, "the more I use my strength, the more I have. I am often much tired the first time I preach in a day; a little the second time; but, after the third or fourth, I rarely feel either weakness or weariness" (IV, 19). The last two volumes of the *Journal* are filled with instances in which Wesley attributed his continued health and service, despite advanced years, to the agency of the Spirit.

So did Wesley affirm God's wisdom and strength in the preaching of the Revival. He was not tempted to credit his successes to his own strength. He stood in wonder at the sight of God's redemptive power. And just as he affirmed that the entire enterprise of preaching was dependent on God, so he affirmed that the response of his hearers was also dependent on the work of the Spirit. He delivered the gospel to his congregations and everything else was between the individual soul and God. His duty was to lead people to God; thereafter they must wrestle with Him. Wesley offers this instruction: "Those whom it pleases God to employ in His work ought to be quite passive in this respect; they should choose nothing, but leave entirely to Him all the circumstances of His own work" (IV, 347f.). Wesley only fears that those who are laid open by the gospel might find an easy escape: "I believe not a few were deeply wounded. Oh may none heal the wound slightly" (V, 204).

In additional entries Wesley makes clear that God is the source of the convincing and saving grace that may accompany preaching: "The house was unusually filled, both with people and with the power of God" (VII, 250). "They contained themselves pretty well during the exhortation; but when I began to pray the flame broke out" (VII, 18). "And now the word of God was as a fire and a hammer. I began again and again, after I thought I had done; and the latter words were still stronger than the former" (III, 363). Toward the close of Wesley's life the response to his preaching again reached great heights. God smote those who heard and brought fruit from seed that had been sown earlier. This eighty-year old had good reason to find deep satisfaction in the great work which he shared and recorded in those days (VII, 244, 266, 396, 435).

Finally, we should note Wesley's readiness to accept the results of his preaching, whether God granted a bountiful harvest or the seed fell on stony soil. He walked four or five miles to preach to a group of people, hoping that doing so would arrest their concern: "But I did not perceive they were at all affected. God only can raise the dead" (V, 314). In another instance he laments, "But I am afraid many of them are sermon-proof" (V, 322). In yet another place he voices his disappointment over the failure of the people to respond: "Both in the morning and evening I spoke as closely and sharply as I could, but yet I cannot find a way to wound the people. They are neither offended nor convinced" (V, 119). He is not pleased with a "stupid" congregation that shows "absolute unconcern." He calls them a "rude, gaping, staring, rabble" (III, 378, 88). On occasion he reluctantly admits, "I could not find the way to their hearts. The generality of the people here are so wise that they need no more knowledge, and so good that they need no more religion! Who can warn them that are brimful of wisdom and goodness to flee from the wrath to come" (VI, 20).

Wesley tried diligently to reach his congregations and he cared very much when they failed to respond to the gospel. But he seemed more concerned for their souls than for his own lack of success. He cast his bread upon the waters and trusted the results to God. After he had done all that he could, he relied on the Spirit to do the effective work in changing the human heart. Undaunted by failure, he moved on to other fields, where the Spirit might reap a better harvest. The *Journal* is remarkably free of suggestions that Wesley spent much time searching within himself for the reasons of his congregations' unresponsiveness. He appears fully able to leave them to God's keeping, his confidence in God unshaken. When God chooses the tide will turn, this Wesley believes, and in this he rejoices: "I preached about noon at Tadcaster with an uncommon degree of freedom, which was attended with a remarkable blessing. A glorious work is dawning here against which nothing can prevail" (VI, 114).

Through the *Journal* we have learned several things about Wesley's preaching and its role in the Revival: He preached incessantly for more than half a century under the most varied circumstances. He scorned no means that promised access to needy souls. He preached the gospel in its fullness, as he understood it, and urged others to do the same. He attributed the heartening response of his audience to the work of the Holy Spirit and committed those who resisted to the care of that same Spirit.

Less clear, and more difficult to determine, are his private thoughts and feelings about his preaching and its impact. Even in these matters, however, many *Journal* entries suggest that his concern for his hearers was honest and deeply rooted; that his preaching was rarely, if ever, an instrument for self-inflation or a weapon for use against others; and that his satisfaction in the successes of the Revival was based not on what he had done, but on what God had done through him and others. In his preaching of the gospel, Wesley exhibited many of the marks of apostleship.

5
The Offense of
the Gospel

The congregations mentioned in the pages of Acts and the *Journal* did not always press forward to assure their preacher that they "enjoyed" his sermon. Such cheerful responses were rare among the members of the congregations who listened to Paul or Wesley setting forth the gospel of the crucified Christ. If we are to believe St. Paul, the gospel is foolishness and a stumbling-block to men and women, who consequently often rejected it with passion—a fact to which Paul frequently referred as he recited the hardships he suffered in the course of his apostleship.

Both Paul and Wesley proclaimed the good news of God's act in Christ for the salvation of the race. More often than not, their preaching evoked abundant and extremely varied responses in their hearers, who were as likely to start a riot as a revival. Many reacted as though the Good News they heard was in fact bad news. Hearing the proclamation of the Cross, they were scandalized and quick to denounce and silence it. On the face of it, it is strange, is it not, that so many were so often offended by the offer of new life in Christ made by Paul and Wesley?

Though Wesley's experiences were no match for those of Paul, he was no stranger to trials and tribulations, which ranged from the antagonism of individuals to the violence of mobs. Page after page of the *Journal* recounts these incidents. Before we examine them to learn their significance in Wesley's thinking, let us consider some perennial and related issues.

Christianity has always offended a great many people for a number of different reasons. Some are offended by petty portrayals of the gospel, which are irrelevant to their needs; some by the chasm between the profession and the practice of its exponents; some by the sugary sentiments in which the gospel is clothed and presented; some by the believers' blind devotion to it, which both scorns and outrages reason.

The *Journal* gives us little reason to believe that Wesley offended people in these ways or by his person or manner. At any rate, these reactions to the distorted proclamation of the gospel can scarcely be made the responsibility of the gospel itself. Further, they fail to explain the opposition that arises when the gospel is preached in its fullness.

How then are we to account for the resistance, ridicule, and persecution that were Wesley's lot for many years? Could the gospel itself be causing the offense? Is there someting at the very heart of the gospel that produces resentment and resistance?

To bring some light to this question, let us examine some *Journal* entries, specifically as they relate to (1) Wesley's characterization of the people who took offense and opposed his work; (2) his accounts of the opposition and violence of those who were offended, and his response; (3) his conviction that offense was rooted in the resistance of the untamed heart to the insistent demands of the Spirit; and (4) his uneasiness when offense gave way to acclamation in the course of the Revival. The *Journal* informs us about Wesley's stand on each of these issues, and about what he made of the offense that so frequently accompanied his preaching of the gospel.

Occasions on which people took offense occurred early and continued through much of Wesley's ministry. From the first, Wesley and the Oxford Methodists were a source of distress. The "Holy Club" that he joined in 1729 was the object of scorn and ridicule. (Because of the carefully regulated behavior of its members, they were called "Methodists" in derision. Slowly they accepted the name that ultimately came to identify the Wesleyan movement (II, 67, 249).) A few years later, as Wesley was still struggling toward Aldersgate, he notes after preaching, "I was afterwards informed, many of the best people were so offended, that I was not to preach there any more" (I, 436).

After Aldersgate, opposition to the preaching of the

Revival increased in frequency and ferocity. Wesley was no longer merely an embarrassing fanatic; he now seemed a fearless herald of God's truth, the more unsettling because he had been set free from preoccupation with himself. He offended nearly everyone, but the offense began in the church among the followers of the Christ; they found his exhortations hard to take. After delivering strong words to one congregation, he remarks, "I fear they will bear me no longer" (II, 76). And again, "As this was the first time of my preaching here, I suppose it is to be the last" (II, 99).

One church after another closed its doors to him and the gospel that he preached, until finally only four churches in all of London admitted him to their pulpit. *Journal* entries noting his exclusion from churches appear again and again (I, 438, 460, 464, 480; II, 144, 533; III, 19, 92, 444, etc.). They crop up as late as 1778, when he writes that a pastor "would not permit me to preach in the church, because it would give offence" (VI, 207)! He admitted, too, that outside the church he sometimes fared little better. Once he was shut out of a meadow in which he proposed to preach by those who opposed his work (II, 193). Elsewhere, he was chastened by neighbors after his congregation had damaged a nearby orchard (II, 244).

Bishops, clergymen, and members of the Church of England were dismayed and discomfited by Wesley, his preaching, and his people. Many dissenting ministers, those who served outside the established church, were likewise offended; some of them excluded from communion anybody who went to hear Wesley (III, 73). Antagonism to Wesley, in his judgment, seemed to be the only thing that bound together Deists and Calvinists, Moravians and Catholics. "I found the roaring lion began to shake himself here also," he reports. "Some Papists, and two or three good Protestant families, were cordially joined together to oppose the work of God; but they durst not yet do it openly, the stream running so strong against them" (III, 349).

The officials at Oxford University also found Wesley hard to bear. As a Master of Arts of the University and as a clergyman in the Church of England, Wesley was invited every three years to preach at St. Mary's before the university body. His ringing sermon immediately after his Aldersgate experience created a stir. Six years later, in 1744, he delivered a still stronger sermon on "Scriptural Christianity," in which he denounced the religious life of the university—the authorities sent for his notes to review them. In his entry in the *Journal* he concludes, "I preached, I suppose the last time, at St. Mary's. Be it so. I am now clear of the blood of these men. I have fully delivered my own soul" (III, 147). His supposition was sound. He was not invited again to take his turn preaching at St. Mary's.

Wesley and the Revival met opposition on yet another front. They were the targets of a fanatical warfare in the press. Wesley ignored many of these attacks as long as he could but was driven on more than one occasion to make an answer. His critics viewed the Revival as a dangerous aberration of the Christian faith, and they endeavored to unmask it and to make its distortions clear. Not only was Wesley attacked in print, he was attacked in person as well. One gentleman, wounded by Wesley's preaching, "began disputing on several heads; and at last told me plainly," Wesley reports, that "one of our own college had informed him they always took me to be a little crack-brained at Oxford" (II, 243). Clearly, Wesley offended many on many occasions.

We need to look next at the vigorous reactions of those who felt offended. Frequently, they not only spoke sharply but also acted decisively. So prevalent was the active opposition, especially in the early years of the Revival, that Curnock entitled part VI of the *Journal* "Perils and Persecutions" (III, 109-269).

Often it was the "good" people, the genteel set, that led the charge, though sometimes not very successfully. One unruly group "lifted up their voice, especially one called a gentleman, who had filled his pockets with rotten eggs; but, a young man coming unawares, clapped his hands on each side, and mashed them all at once. In an instant he was perfumed all over; though it was not so sweet as balsam" (V, 341). Wesley seemed to derive sly satisfaction from the miscarriage of this plan and others, developed by "refined" people who sought to hinder God's work.

Abuse by mobs was common, as we saw in the preceding chapter. These mobs were composed not only of the rabble and chronic troublemakers in a community but of all manner of persons, and their designs could be risky. In one encounter, a mob filled the house in which Wesley desired to preach and "proposed setting it on fire; but one of them, happening to remember that his own house was next, with much ado persuaded them not to do it" (III, 332). Wesley was showered with objects on numerous occasions, and one of his preachers, John Nelson, was severely stoned by an angry mob (III, 290-91; V, 237).

Some of the troublemakers were inventive. Several believers in predestination brought dogs to disrupt one of Wesley's services. "But the dogs were wiser than the men," Wesley observes, "for they could not bring them to make any noise at all." And he adds this laconic remark, "One of the gentlemen supplied their place" (V, 142).

It was indeed a time of widespread peril and persecution. "All this summer," Wesley declares in 1744, "our brethren in the west had as hot service as those in the north of England: the war against the Methodists, so called, being everywhere carried on with far more vigor than against the Spaniards" (III, 150).

Wesley was quite willing to bear the reproach of the

Cross where that was required of him. But he was also determined to claim the rights guaranteed him by English law. Denied the right to preach in one place, he insisted that though the mayor might forbid him, King George did not (III, 494). He appealed to magistrates for redress of the wrongs done him and the movement by individuals and mobs. If a magistrate refused to perform his function, Wesley appealed to higher authorities. "We have both God and the law on our side," he contends, and he was resolved to give up neither one nor the other (V, 151; III, 139, 152, 296, 465; IV, 20, 56, 162). In thus seeking legal redress for the acts of obstruction and violence, he followed the precedent set by St. Paul. Some historians assert that in doing so he significantly strengthened the rule of English law.

Through perils and persecutions, Wesley remained cool and did not waver. Though a small man, he fearlessly stood his ground in the face of threats, aggression, and imminent danger. On one occasion he quieted an unruly crowd by mounting a chair and speaking convincingly to the people (III, 442). On another, after facing down an angry mob, he took his departure with the quiet words, "I wish you good night" (III, 191). On yet another, a mob had "beset the house" where he was and cried, "bring out the minister; we will have the minister." He explains, "I desired one to take their captain by the hand and bring him into the house. After a few sentences interchanged between us the lion became a lamb." Wesley proceeded to calm the rest of the mob whose members turned completely about and became his staunch supporters. He sums up this menacing encounter as follows: "A little before ten, God brought me safe to Wednesbury, having lost only one flap of my waistcoat and a little skin from one of my hands" (III, 98-100).

These incidents and many more of the same kind indicate that Wesley was temperate and purposeful, no matter how precarious the situation. His actions suggest that he felt secure in a power against which human connivance could not ultimately prevail.

How, in fact, did he interpret such intense opposition to his preaching and to the Revival?

Wesley was convinced that much of the resistance he encountered was rooted in satanic forces. He was little troubled by the theological and philosophical problems that accompany belief in Satan; he was much more apprehensive of the powers of darkness, which he detected in the world, wrestling with the souls of his listeners. Thus he writes, "The prince of this world fought with all his might lest his kingdom should be overthrown" (III, 80-81; IV, 325). And again, "A neighboring alehouse-keeper drinks, and laughs, and argues into Deism all the ploughmen and dairymen he can light on. But no mob rises against him; and good reason: Satan is not divided against himself" (IV, 59).

But Satan is not always so shrewd. Wesley is aware of defects in the satanic strategy: "I wonder the devil has not wisdom enough to discern that he is destroying his own kingdom. I believe he has never yet, at any one time, caused this open opposition to the truth of God, without losing one or more of his servants, who were found of God, while they sought Him not" (II, 385). And in yet another place, "A real, deep work of God seemed to be already begun in his soul. Perhaps, by driving him too fast, Satan had driven him to God—to that repentance which shall never be repented of" (III, 239). Finally, he is brought to exclaim, "Satan, thy kingdom hath suffered a loss. Thou fool! How long wilt thou contend with Him that is mightier than Thou?" (II, 393).

Consistently, Wesley saw resistance as the work of evil powers. Locked in a mighty battle with God, these powers had to fight desperately for their existence. Wesley did not wonder at opposition and persecution; to him it was the inevitable defiance by the demonic kingdom of the great work of God.

Not only are Satan and the forces of evil under attack, Wesley contended, but so is sin in the human heart. He recorded some striking examples of the contest between God's grace and man's sin. Preaching at Bath with "some of the rich and great" present, he declares "with all plainness of speech: (1) that, by nature they were all children of wrath; (2) that all their natural tempers were corrupt and abominable; and (3) all their words and works, which could never be any better but by faith; and that (4) a natural man has no more faith than a devil, if so much. One of them, my Lord _____, stayed very patiently till I came to the middle of the fourth head. Then, starting up, he said, ' 'Tis hot! 'tis very hot,' and got downstairs as fast as he could" (III, 65). In a similar situation, Wesley observes, "I could not but take particular notice of one gentleman, who stood as a statue, with his eyes fixed, till the last word of the sermon. Upon inquiry I found he was lord of the manor, and proprietor of the whole town. But he is a sinner. It may be he begins to feel it, and to know that God is no respecter of persons" (VIII, 154).

Wesley believed that sin and pride are laid siege by that most terrible of weapons, the gospel of grace—the offensive, immoral announcement that what we cannot do for ourselves, God has done for us in Christ. And more, that to belong to Christ one must first be broken. Wesley well knew that the way to resurrection with Christ was a difficult, painful death to self. Many experienced this travail in the course of his preaching: "Tears and groans were on every side, among high and low. God, as it were, bowed the heavens and came down. The flame of love went before him; the rocks were broken in pieces, and the mountains flowed down at His presence" (IV, 66). One of the many letters from other persons that Wesley records in the *Journal* includes this striking sentence: "As my mother bore me with great pain, so did I feel great pain in my soul in being born of God" (II, 110). Wesley was neither surprised nor embarrassed by the

61

signs of conflict exhibited by his audience. He was persuaded that one can escape the old sinful self and its
hardened defenses only under the power of God and with
great difficulty and travail.

Time and again, Wesley notes the manifestations of
despair in those with whom the Spirit strives: "Several
began to cry out, in the bitterness of their soul, 'What
must I do to be saved?' " (III, 20). He describes this condition of helplessness as "heaviness" or "settled despair"
(II, 80, 259, 280). He speaks of a "sharp contest" in the
soul and of the cries of those whom the word of God has
"cut to the heart" (II, 294-95, 185). When God's peace
comes, "captives" are "set at liberty" (III, 398). In Wesley's
understanding, despair lay at the heart of the process of
salvation. It marked those who had reached the point
where they had been enabled to "let go and let God." He
knew that the way of despair is neither comfortable nor
easy, neither proud nor painless, and that the needy fight
against it until, in exhaustion, they admit defeat. Wesley
was not disturbed either by resistance or despair; he was
confident that both brought sinners to salvation. He was
most uneasy when all was calm, resistance had died down,
and the gospel had ceased to offend.

This brings us to the final issue we need to address
in Wesley's interpretation of the offense of the gospel. As
the evangelical Revival grew in strength and spread
throughout the land, Wesley began to note a change in
the people and towns he served and a decline in the
persecution and violence that had marked the Revival's
earlier years. At St. Bartholomew he acknowledges how
much the scene has improved in ten years: "Now all are
calm and quietly attentive, from the least even to the
greatest" (III, 356). Years later he remarks, "How is this
town changed! Some years since a Methodist preacher
could not safely ride through it. Now, high and low, few
excepted, say 'Blessed is he that cometh in the name of
the Lord' " (V, 143-44).

The transformation was similar in other places. No longer was there any danger of being met with "a shower of stones" (V, 185). Where Methodist preachers once were thrown into the horse pond, they were now gladly received (VII, 330). Still later, he observes that the people in one place were once "ready to tear any Methodist preacher in pieces. Now not a dog wagged his tongue" (VII, 180). And finally, at the age of eighty-six, he writes, "the last time I was here, above forty years ago,. I was taken prisoner by an immense mob, gaping and roaring like lions. But how is the tide turned! High and low now lined the street, from one end of the town to the other, out of stark love and kindness, gaping and staring as if the King were going by" (VIII, 3).

The dramatic change in the reception given to Wesley and his preachers seems to have surprised and at times disturbed him. At Oxford, in 1751, he writes, "I was much surprised, wherever I went, at the civility of the people—gentlemen as well as others. There was no pointing, no calling of names as once; no, nor even laughter. What can this mean? Am I become a servant of men? Or is the scandal of the cross ceased?" (III, 511-12). In the same mood he writes much later, "I found great liberty of spirit; and the congregation seemed to be much affected. How is this? Do I yet please men? Is the offence of the cross ceased? It seems, after being scandalous near fifty years, I am at length growing into an honourable man" (VI, 137).

Although apparently somewhat pleased, this growing acclaim also made Wesley uneasy. "What have I to do with honour?" he asks, "Lord, let me always *fear,* not *desire* it" (V, 115). To the last the gallant old warrior was suspicious of popularity, even of civil acceptance. Convinced as he was of the offense at the heart of the gospel proclamation, he expected perils and persecutions. They were to him signs that God was at work, and he was often dismayed by their absence. But his dismay was

63

tempered when he considered that open acceptance might also be the work of God: "Here it seems, the scandal of the cross (such is the will of God) is ceased. High and low, rich and poor, flock together, and seem to devour the word" (VII, 363).

How correct is Wesley's view of the offense and the resistance that the gospel produced? That many were offended and that they often struck out in fear and anger is evident from the *Journal* accounts. Further, Wesley seems wholly consistent in his explanation of these events. He asserted over and over again that evil structures were at work in the world and that the tyranny of sin was not easily broken. Faithfully he described the fear and pain that accompanied the struggle against the Spirit before the entry into new life.

Therefore he welcomed the offense of the gospel and was not dismayed that it involved him in peril. He seems to have been able to refer persecution to its real source and not have his confidence and purpose adversely affected by it. He was persuaded that people act in an unaccountable manner when they are under the pressure of the Spirit. He was content to assist their labor in all ways possible, until they came to a new birth. As God's servant, he regarded it as unseemly to ask any more or any better than his Lord had received. His *Journal* record supports the conclusion that, like Paul, he calmly bore the offense of the gospel in full reliance on the grace of God.

6
The Community of the Spirit

In Acts and in the *Journal*, preaching and Christian community are related as are the two sides of a coin. For Paul as for Wesley, preaching aimed to graft into the body of Christ those persons who responded to the invitation of the Spirit. The "solitary" Christian was as much a stranger to one as to the other. For both, preaching was commissioned and carried on by the community of those already possessed by the Spirit. For both, continuation in the life of grace was sustained by fellowship with others who were like-minded. The community-building Spirit was at work where the gospel was duly preached and responded to in faith. The gracious consequence of its work was the gathering of communities of the faithful. In the Book of Acts and in Wesley's *Journal*, the reality and importance of Christian fellowship is everywhere evident. The New Testament church and the "primitive" Wesleyan societies were both expressions of the corporate reality of the Holy Spirit.

From the first days of the church, people the world over have asked questions about its claim to be the fellowship of the Spirit. Is the church truly a necessity for followers of the Christ? Is Christianity primarily a matter of individual faith and life, or is fellowship with others essential to it? Do persons become Christians first and then enter the church, or is the Christian community vital to their entrance into the faith? Does the chronic quarreling, hypocrisy, divisiveness, and struggle for power within the church undercut its claim to be the body of Christ? Does the organization of believers in settled institutions with formal rules and regulations quench the living Spirit? Is it appropriate, in reality, to identify the institutional church with the community of the Spirit? The litany goes on and on. As these questions suggest, the church has been much maligned throughout history, and Wesley himself was often critical of the life of the church of his day and of that of many of its ministers and members.

Perhaps we can sum up the overall thrust of these questions in one brief query: Is Christian community in fact the product of the activity of the Holy Spirit? We will seek Wesley's answer to this question—and by implication his answer to several others we have raised—by reviewing four relevant points: (1) Wesley's conviction that persons do not become or remain Christians apart from the power of the Spirit in the community; (2) his concern for faithfulness to the Spirit in the constitution of community; (3) his freedom in the Spirit to devise measures to build up community life; and (4) his insistence on careful discipline for the maintenance of the community in the power of the Spirit. The *Journal's* constant attention to the many aspects of community life should give us a good idea of Wesley's mind on these matters.

Wesley's work in the Revival was no hit and run affair. He was certain that those made captive by the Spirit through preaching needed intimate fellowship to sustain them. He affirms, "I was more convinced than ever that the preaching like an Apostle, without joining together those that are awakened and training them up in the ways of God, is only begetting children for the murderer" (V, 26). He was not satisfied merely to preach and to convince those who heard him; he also endeavored to organize them into groups in which they might "watch over each other in love"—one of his favorite phrases (III, 430; IV, 316). In his preaching he urged the necessity of Christian fellowship and invited those interested to meet afterwards. In one case, about a hundred persons did so, and to them he "explained the nature of a Christian society, and they willingly joined therein" (VI, 345).

Intimate fellowship offered new followers of the Christian way support for their faith and life. Even so, the road ahead was not easy for them. Wesley cautions, "a huge multitude" heard him gladly, and "seemed to receive the truth in love. I then added about twenty to the little society. Fair blossoms! But how many of these will bring forth fruit" (IV, 450)? He knew all too well that, as many would stray from the narrow path, he had to provide them with every assistance on their journey. Less poetically, he ventures this doleful prediction about one wavering soul: "Surely thus far God has helped him; but, a thousand to one, he will 'return as a dog to his vomit' " (IV, 289).

As a consequence of his concern for those he had won through preaching, Wesley introduced several forms of close Christian fellowship. In Georgia, during the early years of his ministry, he formed "a sort of little Society," whose members met regularly for mutual reproof, instruction, and exhortation (I, 197-205). The model for this group came from the Oxford "Holy Club" and the practice of Moravian congregations. In 1739, in London, he established similar groups that spread rapidly, and the resulting societies became an essential component of the Revival movement.

The societies grew in size as well as in number. By 1742, for example, the society in London had nearly 1,100 members, far too many to realize the fellowship of love and mutual care that Wesley held to be so important. The same year, to discharge a debt on the society's property in Bristol, it was suggested that each member give a penny a week; that groups of twelve be formed within the society; and that leaders be appointed to visit the members of each group to receive their contributions (II, 528, 535). It soon became apparent to Wesley that this structure was providentially suited to meet the needs for which the societies originally had been created: fellowship and faith. Thus another Wesleyan institution came into being: the class meeting.

But even the societies and classes were not enough for Wesley, and he formed other more intimate groups, called bands or select societies. Some of them were composed of men, others of women, and they met to make their confessions of sin and weakness and to press on toward holiness. In one community, for example, three women agreed to meet as did four young men, to confess their faults, to pray together, and to be healed (II, 174).

Many of those who entered these groups were already members of the Church of England—the "established church"—or were "dissenters," adherents of one of the Protestant congregations permitted by English law to exist outside the established church. Many more lived without any connection with any church. However, in bringing these people together in the societies, Wesley had not the slightest intention of founding a new church, as the *Journal* makes abundantly clear. His purpose rather was to revitalize the existing church, whatever its form or profession. He viewed the societies as a sort of "church within the Church," as a leavening influence needed by nearly all Christian communions.

He steadfastly resisted all suggestions that the Methodists "separate" from the Church of England (IV, 114; VII, 422). He encouraged society members to attend the stated services of the church and to take the sacrament there. On the Lord's Day, he regularly attended worship in the established church in which he remained a priest until his death. He would not countenance Methodist services that conflicted with those of the church, except in unusual circumstances. He told rebellious members in one society that they could have service during the church hour if they insisted, but he adds, "remember, from that time you will see my face no more" (VII, 232). Throughout his life, and despite insistence on separation from within the societies and resistance to them from without, he did not qualify his admiration for and loyalty to the historic foundations of the established church (III, 166-67; V, 328; VI, 183; VII, 487).

From the evidence available we may conclude that Wesley intended the societies and their several groups to be adjuncts to the Spirit's work. Quite simply, they were to promote Christian faith and fellowship and be content therewith.

We need now to consider a second aspect of Wesley's understanding of the community of the Spirit, namely, his contention that it must be faithfully constituted. In brief, it must be consistent with the New Testament and the ways of the Spirit. Wesley exhibited lasting interest in the New Testament church—primitive Christianity, as he often called it. For him it was normative for Christian community and he often argued that the marks and manifestations of the Spirit in the societies were like those evident in the congregations of the apostles.

He was well acquainted with and drew upon the early church fathers and the lessons of church history. He was particularly attentive to those factors that he believed had obscured and distorted the realities of primitive Christianity (III, 232). He held that the great councils of the church were subject to error, and he insisted on checking their pronouncements against the Scriptures (I, 275). In this, as in all things, Wesley contended that the written Word of God stand as the sole authority for Christians and the church (III, 26; IV, 317).

He provided a straightforward answer to the problem of standards for admission to the societies: All those are eligible who "desire to flee from the wrath to come." Any other test for participation in them is unnecessary: "I have never read or heard of, either in ancient or modern history, any other Church which builds on so broad a foundation as the Methodists do," he affirms, and "which requires of its members no conformity either in opinions or modes of worship, but barely this one thing, to fear God, and to work righteousness" (VIII, 5).

Admission to Christian community ought not to depend upon correct beliefs or forms of worship but upon the witness that Christ is Lord, made in the power of the Spirit. What was required was the "circumcision of the heart," not the legalistic observance of rituals and duties.

Here as elsewhere Wesley affirmed that this change in the disposition of the heart was the work of God; it was the Spirit that drew the needy into the fellowship of the Christ. The *Journal*, as well as Acts, abundantly testifies to the gracious provenance of the Spirit in claiming persons for Christ and his community.

In another entry, Wesley elaborates this simple test for admission:

> There is no other religious society under heaven which requires nothing of men in order to their admission into it but a desire to save their souls. Look all around you: you cannot be admitted into the Church, or society of the Presbyterians, Anabaptists, Quakers, or any others, unless you hold the same opinions with them, and adhere to the same mode of worship.
>
> The Methodists alone do not insist on your holding this or that opinion; but they think and let think. Neither do they impose any particular mode of worship; but you may continue to worship in your former manner, be it what it may. Now, I do not know any other religious society, either ancient or modern, wherein such liberty of conscience is now allowed, or has been allowed, since the age of the apostles. Here is our glorying; and a glorying peculiar to us. What society shares it with us (VII, 389)?

It would be mistaken to conclude from this that Wesley meant for Methodists to separate from and elevate themselves above other Christians. Whatever their background or tradition, all who met the simple test were welcomed into the societies. Wesley desired Methodism to embody the "Catholic Spirit," that is, the spirit of universal love, and to recognize no boundaries that presumed to confine the work of the Spirit. As has been widely noted, he took the world for his parish. He regarded himself as a "priest of the Church Universal," and thereby "indeterminately commissioned" to preach wherever he might "advance the glory of God and the salvation of souls" (II, 257).

In his eighty-second year, reflecting on the spread of the Revival, Wesley muses, "I was now considering how strangely the grain of mustard-seed, planted about fifty years ago, has grown up. It has spread through all Great Britain and Ireland; the Isle of Wight, and the Isle of Man; then to America from the Leeward Islands, through the whole continent, into Canada and New-foundland" (VII, 59). The advance of Methodism was remarkable to him and frequently he invited all who shared its spirit to join in the work of God made manifest through it (VII, 389).

A third characteristic of the community of the Spirit can be found in Wesley's belief that those commissioned by the Spirit are granted freedom to pursue their task in creative and unusual ways.

Wesley was wedded to the ways of the Church of England and had strong "high church" leanings. He found it difficult to depart from its practices and did so only after reading widely, consulting his Bible, and searching his heart. He knew that new situations demand new measures, or perhaps, the reinstitution of ancient ones, and, further, he was habitually unwilling to deny the prompting of the Spirit. Consequently he struggled with conflicting demands between his traditional inclinations and his reliance on the Spirit. But he found no escape from what he considered to be his distinctive apostolic task. After considering new measures at length, he took needed action reluctantly but resolutely.

His freedom in the Spirit was supported by his interest in Montanus, a second-century charismatic branded heretical by the church. Wesley inclined to view the Montanists as "real scriptural Christians," opposed by insti-

72

tutional leaders because of their full reliance on the Spirit (III, 490).

Wesley's "innovations" form an impressive list. As we have noted, he early began to preach in the fields and highways; his preachers did likewise, and together they propagated the Revival. He employed lay preachers, poorly trained by customary standards and lacking episcopal ordination, certain that they could be effective in the power of the Spirit. As early as 1735 he began free, extemporary preaching instead of reading his sermons or the homilies provided by the church (VI, 96). He allowed and practiced extemporary prayer rather than using the formal liturgies of the church (I, 449; IV, 120). He approved the use of preaching places even though they had not been properly consecrated, contending that the worship of the Spirit provided all the consecration needed (V, 92). As we have seen above, he formed those who had been awakened into distinctive societies, classes, and bands for their nurture in Christian fellowship and love. And in 1784, after much study and reflection, he ordained ministers and a superintendent to administer the sacraments and guide the fortunes of American Methodism (VII, 15).

All these practices Wesley adopted and employed as extraordinary means, as providential aids in the discharge of God's work (V, 79; VII, 160, 486). In 1788, late in life, he sums up these matters, acknowledging "that we have in the course of years, out of necessity, not choice, slowly and warily varied in some points of discipline, by preaching in the fields, by extemporary prayer, by employing lay preachers, by forming and regulating societies, and by holding yearly Conferences." In justification of these actions, he adds, "we did none of these things till we were convinced we could no longer omit them but at the peril of our souls" (VII, 422).

Wesley's reliance on the Spirit, and his conviction that he was called by God to special duties, enabled him to be critical of the established church, to depart from its practices, and to defend his actions when he did so. In Georgia he had once refused communion to a person who lacked baptism by an episcopally ordained minister. Reflecting on this later, he writes, "can anyone carry High Church zeal higher than this? And how well have I been beaten with mine own staff" (III, 434)! In fact, many of the leaders of the church to which he felt such strong loyalty looked on him with suspicion, if not dismay. Some priests in parish churches even kept him away from the sacrament (III, 61-62). In general, they did little to assist and much to complicate his efforts. Undeterred, Wesley pursued his course, confident that God supported it, even if the leaders of the church did not.

Freedom in the Spirit, duly guarded by Scripture, was at the forefront of Wesley's thought and practice. Though it repeatedly brought him and the Methodists under fire, he was not about to surrender what he held to be such an essential element in the community of the Spirit.

One last feature of this community that figures so prominently in Wesley's *Journal* is strict discipline in order to enhance the Spirit's work.

Wesley was nothing if not methodical. From his day to this, Methodists, as their name implies, have valued discipline. Though Wesley stressed the freedom of the Spirit, he also abhorred any prospect of antinomianism, the belief that the Spirit frees believers from all requirements (III, 237; IV, 247). Though he recognized the folly of trying to capture and control the Spirit, he insisted that its providential working was assisted by proper discipline and disrupted by laxity and disorder.

We have already discussed the simple test for admission to the societies. To stay in them, however, once admitted was quite a different matter. In 1743 Wesley published abroad *Rules of the Society for the People Called Methodist,* containing detailed guidance for the conduct of the members of the societies. He urged that they be read frequently in each society and be carefully observed (I, 458; IV, 288; V, 405). He often remarks that, "Those who are resolved to keep these rules may continue with us, and those only" (V, 36). He insisted that his preachers keep and enforce the Rules. When they met in conference in 1756, "The Rules were read over, and carefully considered one by one; but," Wesley notes, "We did not find any that could be spared. So we all agreed to abide by them all, and to recommend them with our might" (IV, 185).

On many occasions, Wesley observed that the decline and deadness of a society was the result of disregard for discipline. He laments, "I met the classes; but found no increase in the society. No wonder, for discipline has been quite neglected; and, without this, little good can be done among the Methodists" (VII, 21). A society that had done well owed its "prosperous condition," he maintains, "to the exact discipline which has for sometime been observed among them . . . and, to the strongly and continually exhorting the believers 'to go on unto perfection' " (VII, 160).

To maintain discipline, Wesley regularly examined the members of the societies (II, 412; IV, 15; V, 98, 289). His concern was not for their hearts, that was God's affair, but for their lives and their conduct (III, 284). Those of whom he approved received tickets of admission to meetings of the classes and societies (II, 479). Those who did not "walk according to the gospel" were excluded from the community until they repented of their offenses (II, 526; III, 144). On a visit to Dublin, for example, he "found it necessary to exclude one hundred and twelve members" for their own good and that of the society (VII, 294).

Wesley believed that this practice was necessary though attended by dangers. In his disciplinary work he endeavored to be patient and kind and to act in love. He

75

emphasizes the point: "Oh how patient, how meek, how gentle toward all men ought a preacher, especially a Methodist, to be" (VII, 277). Acting in this spirit, he recalls, "I laboured to reunite the poor, shattered society, and to remove the numberless offenses which had torn them in pieces" (V, 320, 347). He is confident that good results follow the enforcement of discipline and writes hopefully of a society he had purged, "I trust they will now increase, as the offenses are removed, and brotherly love restored" (V, 423).

Wesley's preachers were not exempt from discipline designed to strengthen the religious community. He warns, "Nothing will stand in the Methodist plan, unless the preacher has his heart and hand in it. Every preacher, therefore, should consider it is not his business to mind this or that thing only, but everything" (V, 419). More specifically, he advises, "(1) Let all the people sacredly abstain from backbiting, tale-bearing, evil-speaking; (2) let all our preachers abstain from returning railing for railing, either in public or in private, as well as from disputing; (3) let them never preach controversy, but plain, practical, and experimental religion" (V, 230).

When the good of the community demanded it, Wesley acted with resolution and firmness. "I heard George Bell once more," he writes, "and was convinced he must not continue to pray at the Foundry. The reproach of Christ I am willing to bear, but not the reproach of enthusiasm if I can help it" (IV, 541). And again, "But I verily believe we are better without William Moore than with him, as his heart is not right with God" (VII, 54). Occasionally, he received a grateful reply from one he had reprimanded, thanking him for the rebuke, confessing wrong-doing, and imploring forgiveness and grace (III, 173). By careful discipline and detailed regulation of the lives of his people, Wesley hoped to expose them to the Spirit, keep them in its power, and assist them in avoiding pitfalls that may snare the unwary.

76

Wesley the disciplinarian also valued statistical data if they were properly interpreted. He was concerned about the numerical growth of the societies and regularly transcribed their membership lists to bring them up to date. "I now inquired particularly whether the societies were increasing or decreasing," he writes, and adds, "I could not hear of a decrease in any" (VI, 170). He often equated a decline in numbers with a fall from grace, but occasionally he viewed reduced numbers as a good thing: "The society, which the first year consisted of above eight hundred members, is now reduced to four hundred; but, according to the old proverb, the half is more than the whole." And he concludes with satisfaction, "We shall not be ashamed of any of these when we speak with our enemies in the gate" (III, 285).

Several times he chided the brethren who padded their conference reports. "Oh, when will even the Methodists learn not to exaggerate?" he asks. "After all the pompous accounts I had had of the vast increase of the society, it is not increased at all; nay, it is a little smaller than it was three years ago" (VI, 188; III, 338). He was concerned about numbers as they represent people, but he was not entranced by figures. When he found increases in a society, he often adds this observation, "Increased, I hope, in grace as well as in number" (VII, 210).

What then can we say about Wesley's view of the community of the Spirit? In his *Journal* he defended and embodied his conviction that this community is requisite for Christian faith and life; that it is vibrant only in the power of the Spirit; that the person chosen by the Spirit to head the community is led into uncharted ways; and that careful attention to discipline within the community is indispensible for its continuation in the Spirit.

In these ways and for these purposes, Wesley believed the Spirit had called communities of Methodists into being. Through the Revival, Christian community had been renewed across the length and breadth of the

77

land. A nation bore the mark of the Revival, and tributes to John Wesley increased in number and adulation. But their recipient knew himself to be only an unprofitable servant, whom God in his goodness had seen fit to use.

Another Journal Entry

Penne, France   June 1982

Mon. 21—I have spent considerable time with John Wesley's impressive *Journal*. I want to set down some reflections, before they escape me, on what I have read.

At times during my study I have had doubts about my interpretation of Wesley's pages. Perhaps I imposed my own predilections on his material. Perhaps the *Journal* is focused more on human response than on divine initiative, and I have misrepresented it. Perhaps, too, in time I will resolve these and other uncertainties; but for the present, I am committed to the approach I have taken.

My reading has raised other issues; most important, What relevance does the *Journal* have for my generation? This question has come up repeatedly and I have tried to put the lessons contained in the entries into everyday language and to determine their meaning for us today. This is what I make of the four primary themes I have explored as I tried to look at the *Journal* as illustrative of divine initiative.

1. I am impressed by Wesley's consistent testimony to the power of love as the effective agent in nearly everything he records. For some of us, such testimony might be suspect. For Wesley, it seems both honest and deeply felt. For him, God's love was in truth the moving force in all human effort to actualize the good. I find it difficult to dispute this belief.

2. Again, in the *Journal* Wesley stresses a love that insistently reaches out to the unloved, to those who are most in need. Love seeks to meet us in our loneliness and estrangement. It offers acceptance to all, even to those of us who think we do not need it. In broadest terms, isn't this what "preaching"—the offer of love—is all about?

3. *Journal* accounts of resistance to the gospel seem to address each one of us. The approach of love threatens the protective barriers we have erected, and we feel compelled to struggle against it to preserve our accustomed ways of life. The pursuit of love offends us because it unveils our innermost secrets, uncovers our subtle evasions, and challenges our

proud pretensions. That which we most need, we most desperately try to escape, and we are often violent in our rejection.

4. Finally, the *Journal* witnesses to the persistence of a love that breaks through our resistance, overcomes our estrangement, and brings us into loving community. Love reconstitutes on a new basis our relationships to God, neighbor, and self. Through the power of love we become what, at a deeper level, we were created to be—children of God! Is this not the meaning of becoming new creatures, part of the body of Christ?

I was surprised that in this process of transformation, I discovered realities similar to those formulated in trinitarian doctrine. As Father, God reaches out in love to His estranged creatures. As the Son—pure love among us—He compels us to confront our estrangement, and we retreat, resist, and do violence; love suffers crucifixion. As Holy Spirit, undefeated love heals our broken relationships and makes us whole. Most simply, I would characterize this threefold pattern as the initiative, the travail, and the triumph of Love. I am aware that these brief suggestions lack theological profundity and may entail serious theological problems. But they are meaningful to me now as I reflect on Wesley's *Journal.*

Robert E. Chiles

Part Two

THE LETTERS
Epistles of
Apostolic Concern

"You are all partakers with me of grace, both in my imprisonment and in the defense and confirmation of the gospel."

Philippians 1:7 (RSV)

Few figures in Christian history have more in common with St. Paul than does John Wesley. Both were proud of their ancestry and were devout supporters of their time-honored religious traditions. Both possessed unusual insight and ability and were well prepared for their appointed tasks. Both struggled to gain God's acceptance through works of righteousness and knew the futility of their most strenuous efforts. Both were turned sharply about by climactic "conversion" experiences that freed them to enter lifelong contests for souls.

Paul and Wesley were devoted apostles of Jesus Christ. They served Him long and well, frequently under adverse circumstances. For Him they suffered perils and persecution; they rejoiced that their work flourished despite, and sometimes because of, the resistance to it. They were content to do His bidding in the midst of uncertainty and conflict.

Paul and Wesley were apostles to the Gentiles, that is, to all who lacked faith and stood outside the kingdom. Their extensive travels and missionary journeys tell us much about their ingenuity and persistence as heralds of God's kingdom. They excluded no one from the concerns of an apostleship that was limited only by time and space, and the assaults they made on those limits are astounding.

Both were also builders of the church. Their preaching gave rise to communities of Christ in scattered places. They felt responsible for their congregations, and to their preaching they added pastoral and disciplinary duties. When they were detained from visiting their congregations, they sent messengers or letters—sometimes both.

Obviously Wesley's *Letters* cannot be equated with those of Paul. But they can be used to develop a model for apostleship not unlike that in Paul's epistles, and their main characteristics can be summed up as follows: (1) they examine critically the credentials of the apostle; (2) they testify to Wesley's defense of fundamental doctrines while remaining tolerant of mere opinions; (3) they report his enforcement of the reality of the gospel against illusion and pretense; and (4) they manifest his pervasive concern that Christian faith should find fulfillment in Christian practice. These marks of apostleship are discussed in each of our final four chapters.

By any standard, John Wesley's ministry was remarkably productive. Its secret seems to have been that it was rooted in grace, inspired by gratitude, and expressed in love. Like the epistles of Paul, Wesley's *Letters* portray a man who preached, served, lived, and died in "the defense and confirmation of the gospel."

7
The Call of John Wesley

God's call often comes in unexpected and dramatic ways. So it came to St. Paul, and so it came to John Wesley. The lives of both were arrested in mid-course and turned sharply about as they became servants of the reconciling Christ. They rejoiced in their newfound freedom, even as they trembled in their appointments.

In submitting to their call St. Paul and Wesley took on great and urgent responsibilities that far exceeded their powers to perform. In discharging their mission they ventured into new and untried paths, sustained by the providence to which they had surrendered. They willingly accepted criticism and abuse, trusting their cause to God. Now and again they were moved to defend and justify their apostleship by pointing to the changes that God had wrought through them. Neither, however, allowed the misgivings or censure of others or the difficulty of the task to deflect him from the appointed duty.

Wesley might well be offended by my effort to compare his ministry to the apostleship of St. Paul. He explicitly denied all aspirations to such a vaunted role. Yet there is much in his *Letters* to warrant my proposition. They make clear his thoughts on his ministry, its basis, purpose, and power, and they show how he transformed his thoughts into action.

For the moment, though, let us put aside the conception of apostleship and direct our attention to ministers of the gospel—a subject about which many questions have been raised. For example: By what authority does a fallible human presume to instruct others in the ways of God? How does one determine if a "call" derives from God rather than from one's determination or imagination? What qualifications and preparation fit a person for God's work? How does one avoid self-righteousness, overconfidence, and the pursuit of personal ambition in this mission? How does one escape feelings of self-doubt, resentment, and hostility when under criticism and attack? Is it appropriate to justify one's mission, and if so by what means? Must a minister be apologetic and diffident after exerting every effort for the good of the cause?

Wesley appears to have contended with these and still more perplexities surrounding his calling and, in the course of his long ministry, to have come to terms with most of them. What he concluded, therefore, should be relevant to the frequently asked questions and to our purpose in this chapter. We can group his conclusions as they appear in his *Letters* according to four related subjects: (1) his convictions about the call and the credentials of the apostle; (2) his understanding of the responsibilities an apostleship entails; (3) his certainty that criticism and abuse will be the lot of the true servant of God; and (4) his efforts to justify his call by appealing to the changes in human life that God effected through him.

We can scarcely begin our account of Wesley's call with details of an early reprobate existence, for his life was a model of deportment. His upbringing was strongly influenced by devout parents, whose religious instruction and moral example he followed through his childhood and university study. After assisting in his father's parish at Epworth, he returned to Lincoln College at Oxford and in 1729 joined the "Holy Club" in which his brother Charles was a leader (I, 124ff.). Holiness became his goal, and he worked at its attainment with methodical devotion and effort (I, 47, 114). In his two years in Georgia, his goal was the same, though differently phrased. My "chief motive," he says, is the "hope of saving my own soul" (I, 188).

But holiness eluded him, as did the happiness that he believed it would bring. He was still an "almost Christian." At Aldersgate on May 24, 1738, all this changed, and he found peace and satisfaction. He was grasped by the truth that he had tried to believe and had begun to preach: "By grace we are saved through faith." Like Paul, he had been devoutly religious from his early years; like him also, his works had been many and zealously pursued, but they had not resulted in the assurance of salvation. His had been the faith of a servant, not that of a son (I, 262-64). Damascus and Aldersgate, however, placed both apostles in God's hands in a radical way. Their newfound faith stilled their anxious hearts, gave them a new authority, laid on them a far-reaching commission, and empowered them in its keeping.

The call to apostleship, Wesley believed, is from God, who grants the faith that it requires. He asserted that his calling did not rest on his merit but rather on the grace of God. He was keenly aware of his unworthiness and referred to himself as a "worm," a "dead dog," quite insufficient for the task (II, 265). Earlier, in anticipation of the calling, he writes, "It is not for me, who has been a grievous sinner from my youth up, and am yet laden with foolish and hurtful desires; to expect God should work so great things by my hands; but I am assured, if I be once fully converted myself, He will then employ me both to strengthen my brethren and to preach His name to the Gentiles, that the very ends of the earth may see the salvation of our God" (I, 190). During his fifty years of service this is exactly what he did.

Wesley understood God's call to be urgent and consuming. In his early years, when he struggled to find God, or rather struggled to be found by God, he notes, "Leisure and I have taken leave of one another: I propose to be busy as long as I live" (I, 34). In the early months of the Revival, he declined an invitation, saying, "Till our gracious Master sendeth more labourers into His harvest, all my time is much too little." (I, 262). Much later, reflecting on his years of service, he admits, "I have given up all my worldly hopes, my friends, my reputation," in order to promulgate the gospel, "for which I have so often hazarded my life, and by the grace of God will do again" (V, 274).

Those who are called have no time for frivolous pursuits, as Wesley makes clear in this admonition to one so inclined: You "thought of taking a little sport, and catching a few fish or killing a partridge or an hare. Miserable employment for a preacher of the gospel! for a Methodist preacher, above all others" (III, 142). That Wesley himself had no part in frivolous activities is borne out by the record. He traveled 250,000 miles by horse and by carriage and preached 40,000 sermons in the course of his active ministry!

Wesley desired those called by God both to equip and to deport themselves so as to serve the community of the Spirit as effectively as possible. And while he insisted that his preachers should bend every effort to acquire useful knowledge, he cautioned that learning Latin and Greek are not as important as serving Christ. He warns, too, "Beware you be not swallowed up in books; an ounce of love is worth a pound of knowledge" (V, 110, 359). Again, he admonishes several of his preachers, "Scream no more, at the peril of your soul. . . . Speak with all your heart, but with a moderate voice." And he cites his own example, "I often speak loud, often vehemently; but I never scream, I never strain myself. I dare not; I know it would be a sin against God and my own soul" (VI, 167; VIII, 190).

Those summoned by God are not immune to doubts and temptations about their call. To one anxious preacher Wesley writes, "At present you are exactly in your place; and I trust no temptation, inward or outward, should ever induce you to depart from the work, to which God has called you. You must expect to be pushed to both extremes by turns—self-confidence and too much diffidence. But it is certain the former is the more dangerous of the two; and you need all the power of God to save you from it. And He will save you to the uttermost, provided you still retain the sense of your poverty and helplessness" (V, 191).

The call of an apostle entails heavy responsibilities; God's initiative does not eliminate but demands human responsiveness. In correspondence with one of his preachers, Wesley defines this responsibility: "You have one business on earth—to save souls," he writes, "give yourself wholly to this. . . . Pursue the whole of scriptural Christianity. Stand upon the edge of this world, ready to take wing; having your feet on earth, and your eyes and heart in heaven" (III, 148). Ministers who fail to meet this exacting charge are regarded as "blind leaders of the blind." At one point he enters this indictment: "A lifeless, unconverting minister is the murderer-general of his parish. He enters not into the kingdom of heaven himself, and those that would enter in he suffers not. He stands in the gap between them and true religion. Because he has it not, they are easy without it" (II, 95-96; III, 151).

Those who respond to the call in faith have the whole earth before them. Dispatching George Shadford to preach in the new world, Wesley writes, "I let you loose, George, on the great continent of America. Publish your message in the open face of the sun, and do all the good that you can" (VI, 23). And in the same vein he talks about his own work: "If I live till spring, and should have a clear, pressing call, I am as ready to embark for America as for Ireland. All places are alike to me. . . . Wherever the work of our Lord is to be carried on, that is my place for today. And we live only for today; it is not our part to take thought for tomorrow" (V, 212).

In the discharge of his responsibilities, Wesley relied for vision and guidance on the Spirit, as we have seen in the previous chapter. In the *Letters* he sounds the same theme: "It is plain to me that the whole work of God termed Methodism is an extraordinary dispensation of His providence. Therefore I do not wonder if several things occur therein which do not fall under the ordinary rules of discipline" (V, 257; II, 233ff.). He justified the use of lay preachers who had an extraordinary call and viewed itinerant preaching and field preaching as special means particularly suited to the needs of the time (II, 96). In a well-known letter to Vincent Perronet on the history and development of Methodism, Wesley summarized the measures he had devised to carry on the work of God: classes; watch nights; quarterly reviews of members; formation of bands and select societies; and utilization of class leaders, assistants, and stewards. All these and more he took to be part of God's purpose for Methodism. Whatever supplied the want of the gospel, he maintained, should be seized upon and used.

He believed that separation from the established church would result in great loss, but that was not his deepest anxiety. "I only fear the preachers' or the people's leaving not the church but the love of God and inward or outward holiness," he confesses (III, 132). He admits that, "soul-damning clergymen lay me under more difficulties than soul-saving laymen" (III, 151). Despite some trepidation, he ordained ministers for service in America, arguing that his action was in accord with scriptural practice (VII, 238, 262, 284). He was not frightened by predictions of long-range calamity stemming from his practices: "I am not careful for what may be an hundred years hence. He who governed the world before I was born shall take care of it likewise when I am dead. My part is to improve the present moment" (II, 94).

Wesley knew that the gospel induced opposition and caused its heralds to be attacked. He knew that the apostle's confidence in his call, his freedom to modify and to innovate new measures, and his success in the work of salvation would arouse resistance and resentment. In chapter 5, we explored his accounts in the *Journal* of the offense of the gospel. In the *Letters,* he reports of antagonism directed openly and sharply at himself.

Attacks on Wesley's person and activities had begun at Oxford, where he and other members of the "Holy Club" were widely ridiculed. In addition to "Methodists," a term that endured, they were called "The Reforming Club," "The Godly Club," "The Enthusiasts," "Supererogation Men," and "Sacramentarians" (I, 123-33). But Wesley then hoped to gain from this criticism. "A fair exchange," he writes, "if by the loss of reputation we can purchase the least degree of purity" (I, 37). Later he seems to have given up the hope that he would gain from enduring hardship and entered no claims against God for his sufferings.

The spread of the Revival added to the volume and venom of attacks on it and on him. Some critics vigorously assailed Wesley and his movement in letters, print, and public speech. A few, like John Baily and Dr. Free, were quite scurrilous in their condemnation (III, 286ff.; IV, 30ff.). Wesley was understandably loath to have his work misunderstood and maligned. He protests one severe indictment made by Dr. Gibson, Bishop of London, in these words: "Could your Lordship discern no other enemies of the gospel of Christ? Are there no other heretics or schismatics on earth, or even within the four seas? Are there no Papists, no Deists in the land? Or are their errors of less importance?" (II, 287, 330ff.).

Wesley often warns those to whom he advances spiritual counsel: "Never imagine you can be 'faithful to your trust' without offending anybody. Regard not that; follow your own conscience without fear of favour. Do the best you can, and you do enough! 'Angels can do no more' " (VII, 38). "Almost Christians" will harass those who devoutly live practical Christianity (V, 154). This is to be expected, for persecution is the lot of Christians wherever their lot is cast (I, 211, 367).

But antagonism and persecution were not all loss. As we have seen, Wesley was wary of acceptance or acclaim, fearing such favor meant he had compromised the gospel. These difficulties, he alleged, could be a good thing. "At present," he laments, "we have rather too little than too much persecution. We have scarce enough to keep us awake" (VII, 178). From experience he could report, "I have seen more make shipwreck of the faith in a calm than in a storm. We are apt in sunshiny weather to lie down and sleep; and who can tell what may be done before we awake?" (III, 87).

Wesley was compelled to defend and justify his work in the face of these criticisms. Those who chose to dispute his calling received an assured answer. "My extraordinary call," he explains, "is witnessed by the works God doeth by my ministry, which prove that He is with me of a truth in this exercise of my office" (I, 322). Though he refused to claim the powers that distinguished the first apostles, he admits that he prays for signs and wonders of a particular kind: "The conversion of sinners; the 'healing the broken in heart; the turning men from darkness to light, from the power of Satan unto God' " (IV, 40). Those who inquired "whether a pretense to an immediate mission to preach ought not to be confirmed by miracles?" he confidently assures, "Yes, by the grand miracle of saving sinners from their sins" (III, 93). The test of the calling of a minister lies in what God accomplishes through him, not in his qualifications or position (II, 146ff.). On many occasions Wesley reiterated this pragmatic justification of his calling and work. He argued that the stamp of validity is placed on preaching and Christian community as both bring souls from the power of Satan to the power of God (II, 75ff.); and further, that lay preachers, though lacking ordination, prove their calling by saving the lost (V, 249).

In his appeal to the "facts" of changed lives, abundantly manifest in the Revival, Wesley confounded his critics. They could accuse him of peculiarities, authoritarianism, and overzealousness, but they were hard put to dismiss the Revival as the product of his vanity or sheer illusion.

With some confidence we can now summarize Wesley's understanding of his call. First, it is a commission from God apart from one's own capacity or resolve; second, those who follow in the apostolic tradition commit themselves fully and finally to a life of unreserved activity under the direction of the Spirit; third, the call exposes an apostle to criticism and attack rather than exempting him from such treatment; and fourth, one effectively called by God can "boast," as did Paul, of the fruits of his labors, assured that they are not his own but God's work. In these aspects, persons who share the apostolic calling exhibit a dignity born of grace. Wesley's *Letters* strongly support the view that he became a man of poise and presence through his call to a great work that prospered in the power of God, who had summoned and sent him forth.

8
The Defense of the Gospel

St. Paul gave us a profound and decisive understanding of the Christian faith that was exemplified in his work. He found it necessary to protect the sense of the gospel from dilution and distortion, not for theoretical reasons but for the sake of Christian life and community. For him theology was the formulation and articulation of the redemptive realities meant to assist the working of the Spirit. Surely few would ascribe to Paul the "think and let think" attitude that has been applied to Wesley for many years.

Wesley was not the creative and formative thinker that Paul was. No one can replace Paul's understanding of the Christian faith; later generations must inescapably reckon with his materials, whatever they might choose to do with them. However, all this does not mean that Wesley had little of consequence to say in the realm of theology—he probably had more to say than Methodists have been willing to hear.

Paul and Wesley were not only practical preachers and passionate missionaries, they were also careful thinkers who endeavored to relate the faith to important aspects of Christian life and community. To make a distinction between preachers and theologians is perhaps misleading. The two roles imply and require one another so that to separate them could result in a loss. If Paul managed to do justice to both roles, can we not assume that Wesley might have done likewise? Can we not then regard Wesley, in his own time and manner, as a "defender of the faith"?

It is true that Methodism's only "Institutes," vaguely similar to those of Calvin, were written not by Wesley but by a second generation British Wesleyan, Richard Watson. Wesley was not a professional theologian interested in training Christian leaders by lecture and literature. But neither was he an armchair observer, unacquainted with the dust of the arena. He was, above all, an involved, effective preacher. If, in addition, he

held the understanding of the basic realities of the faith
to be of great importance, and if his life and ministry
bear witness to this conviction, then, perhaps we can
make a case for him as a defender of the faith.

To arrive at a reasoned judgment about Wesley's
understanding and support of theology, let us examine
several important facets of his work: (1) his reluctant but
significant participation in controversial writing; (2) his
oft-repeated and disparaging statements about "mere
opinions" in religion; (3) his careful attention to Christian
orthodoxy, its traditional expressions, and its distortions
in his day; and (4) his insistence on the "old Methodist
doctrines," on imposed standards of belief, and on the
subordination of both to Christian love. The results should
clarify Wesley's perspective on each of these issues and
on the broader subject to which this chapter addresses
itself.

Let us look first at Wesley's involvement in "controversial" writing. He was no eager contestant, alert for
occasions on which to defend the gospel. He had more
important things to do. He testifies, "I mean this; every
hour I have is employed more to the glory of God. Therefore, if short answers to opponents will not suffice, I cannot help it; I will not, I cannot, I dare not spend any more
time in that kind of writing than I do" (IV, 118; V, 339-40).
The same reluctance to slight his primary calling is evident in this rejoinder: "It might be worth while for another man to dispute these points with you. But for me
it is not. I am called to other work; not to make Church
of England men or Baptists, but Christians, and men of
faith and love" (III, 37). He advises another on controversial writing: "Have a particular care that they do not
take up too much either of your time or your thoughts.
You have better work: keep to your one point, Christ
dying for us and living in us" (VIII, 69).

Not only may controversy divert a minister from his
true task but it also has dangers, as Wesley knew, and in

the end was relatively ineffective. One of the dangers that he feared was the loss of compassion. He was afraid, he confesses, "not of my adversary, but of myself. I fear my own spirit, lest 'I fall where many mightier have been slain.' I never knew one (or but one) man write controversy with what I thought a right spirit. Every disputant seems to think, as every soldier, that he may hurt his opponent as much as he can: nay, that he ought to do his worst to him. . . . But not to despise him, or endeavour to make others do so, is quite a work of supererogation" (II, 212-13). To one of his colleagues, he writes: "I commend you for meddling with points of controversy as little as possible. It is abundantly easier to lose our love in that rough field than to find the truth" (V, 304). Too often he had himself experienced this common lack of charity.

Moreover, Wesley was sensitive to the temptations of reason and argument and to the basic fruitlessness of controversy. He frequently warns his correspondents about undue preoccupation with reason: "You are a great deal less happy than you would be if you did not reason too much. This frequently gives that subtle adversary an advantage against you. You have need to be continually as a little child, simply looking up for whatever you want" (VI, 243). And on the inadequacy of argument: "In spite of all my logic *I cannot so prove* any one point in the whole compass of Philosophy or Divinity as not to leave room for strong objections," he acknowledges. "But if I could, my answer, however guarded, will give room to equally strong objections. And in this manner, if the person is a man of sense, answers and objections may go on *in infinitum*" (IV, 181; III, 104; VII, 319).

Though a reluctant combatant, Wesley did engage in an extensive defense of the Christian faith. In editing Wesley's *Letters*, Telford selected, and had printed in smaller type at the back of Volumes II through V, fourteen longer letters, which he entitled "Controversial Correspondence." Similar letters make up two-thirds of Volume II, which covers a particularly active period in the Revival—the years 1742 to 1749. Volume IV of the *Letters* is filled with rebuttals addressed to the editors of various publications that had carried articles attacking Wesley and Methodism. The *Letters* also include many private messages in which Wesley explains and defends his thoughts and work. It also bears mentioning that the longest single writing from Wesley's pen was his closely reasoned critique of John Taylor's treatise on *The Doctrine of Original Sin* (IV, 66ff.).

Obviously, Wesley was able to overcome his misgivings about controversial writing on more that one occasion. "I have neither inclination nor leisure to draw the saw of controversy," he asserts, then relents a bit, "but I will tell you my mind in a few words" (VII, 262). In 1778 he indicates that he should have offered more opposition to Calvinism: "I have done this too seldom, scarce once in fifty sermons: I ought to have done it once in fifteen or ten" (VI, 295). Yet he rarely lost sight of his true end and admonishes all, "We must *build* with one hand while we fight with the other" (V, 344).

It is not necessary, however, to feel sorry for this halting champion of the faith; he more than holds his own! His letters bear witness to the mastery he had gained through his work as a tutor at Lincoln College. To a charge made by Mr. Church that Wesley believed lacked sufficient proof, he retorts, "I can look upon this assertion as no other than a flourish of your pen" (II, 228, 348). And more sharply he levels his accusation against another tormentor: "You made a furious attack on a large body of people, of whom you knew just nothing. Blind and bold, you laid about you without fear or wit, without any regard either to truth, justice, or mercy. And thus you entertained both morning and evening a large congregation who came to hear 'the words of eternal life' " (V, 244). About one notorious opponent Wesley writes: "Mr. Augustus Toplady I know well. But I do not fight with chimney-sweepers. He is too dirty a writer for me to meddle with. I should only foul my fingers" (V, 192). And he slyly rebukes another adversary, "Judge, therefore, if they do well who throw me into the ditch, and then beat me because my clothes are dirty" (IV, 145)! Though unwilling to be drawn into controversy, when he did engage in it he did so effectively, always sensitive to its temptations and dangers.

But now, what about Wesley's many words on "mere opinion," and his stress on the disposition of the heart as the only thing needful? Right opinions, Wesley says repeatedly, are "at best a very slender part of religion" (II, 293). "Whoever agrees with us in that account of practical religion given in *The Character of a Methodist,* I regard not what his other opinions are, the same is my brother and sister and mother. I am more assured that love is of God than that any opinion whatsoever is so" (II, 34). In that account he pronounced the often quoted words that seem so contrary to his insistence on orthodox belief: "Is thy heart right, as my heart is with thine? I ask no further question. If it be, give me thine hand."

And further on he adds to this impression in these words: "In public speaking speak not one word against opinions of any kind. We are not to fight against notions but sins" (II, 110). The Revival, he further asserts, attempted a "reformation, not of opinions (feathers, trifles not worth the naming), but of men's tempers and lives; of vice in every kind; of everything contrary to justice, mercy, or truth" (VI, 61; II, 279ff.).

Another source of the conviction that Wesley was indifferent to belief is his reiterated statement of the basis for admission to the societies. Only "one condition" is required of seekers, " 'a desire to flee from the wrath to come, to be saved from their sins' " (II, 294). His well-known sermon on the "Catholic Spirit" is yet another source of Methodist views on Wesley's tolerance of belief.

But it is important to note his comments on that sermon. "From the text of that sermon I do not infer that Christians should not inquire into each other's opinions," he affirms. Methodists should "all desire to be of a catholic spirit; meaning thereby, not an indifference to all opinions, not an indifference as to modes of worship: this they know to be quite another thing." He makes clear that his purpose is not to encourage indifference, but love. "Catholic love is a catholic spirit" (III, 182, 13).

The primary issue is this: Does Wesley view all statements about Christian faith merely as opinions, or does he see opinions as referring more to the peripheral matters of belief? Is Wesley himself committed to the basic truths of the gospel and insistent that others be orthodox also? A distinction in the relative importance of doctrines seems clearly suggested in his reply to a charge of "distinguishing away" the truth. "When men tack absurdities to the truth of God with which it has nothing to do," he remarks, "I distinguish away those absurdities and let the truth remain in its native purity" (II, 90). And he implies that the Scriptures provide guidance in separating less from more important matters: "I am not fond of any opinions as such. I read the Bible with what attention I can, and regulate all my opinions thereby to the best of my understanding" (III, 167).

Wesley's commitment to orthodoxy can be seen in this declaration: "No singularities are my most beloved opinions; that no singularities are more, or near so much, insisted on by me as the general, uncontroverted truths of Christianity" (II, 49). He also desired to demonstrate his agreement with the theology of the Church of England, the Reformation, and above all, with biblical revelation.

His faith, he affirms, does not differ from but rather is a true rendering of the faith of the Church of England, his doctrines are no other "than the genuine doctrines of the Church as expressed both in her Articles and Service"

(II, 233). Elsewhere he contends, "The Methodists, so called, observe more of the Articles, Rubrics, and Canons of the Church than any other people in the three kingdoms. They vary from none of them willingly" (VI, 28). Wesley makes this point again and again against his clerical opponents in the established church.

Many times he asserts his essential continuity with the Protestant Reformation. Methodists, he reports, are often judged "heterodox in several points, and maintainers of strange opinion. And the truth is, the old doctrines of the Reformation are now quite new in the world. Hence those who revive them cannot fail to be opposed by those of the clergy who know them not" (III, 291). He claims no innovations: "We aver it is the one old religion," to which we are devoted, "as old as the Reformation, as old as Christianity, as old as Moses, as old as Adam" (IV, 131). That is how new and different Wesley took Methodism to be! His attachment to the Reformation was not absolute, however. He writes, "I love Calvin a little, Luther more; the Moravians, Mr. Law, and Mr. Whitefield far more than either. . . . But I love truth more than all" (II, 25).

The utlimate test of orthodoxy is the Scriptures. "If I am a heretic," Wesley confesses, "I became such by reading the Bible. All my notions I drew from thence; and with little help from men, unless in the single point of Justification by Faith" (IV, 216). And again, "the Scriptures are a complete rule of faith and practice; and they are clear in all necessary points. And yet their clearness does not prove that they need not be explained, nor their completeness that they need not be enforced" (II, 325). He counsels a seeker after truth, "All that you want to know of Him is contained in one book, the Bible. Therefore your one point is to understand this. And all you learn is to be referred to this, as either directly or remotely conducive to it" (IV, 247, 369; V, 313; VI, 123; VII, 251).

Wesley's orthodox inclinations are further evident in

his criticism of mystics, Calvinists, Socinians, Deists, Antinomians, and others he believed to have compromised the faith. Mystics he first met in William Law. Though he appreciated Law's help, he criticizes Law for leading him to "slight any of the means of grace" (I, 207, 239-40; III, 361ff.). Wesley struggled for years with the Calvinists and their insistence on the doctrine of predestination, never yielding a point. He did, however, hold his Methodist colleague, George Whitefield, in high esteem despite his Calvinist leanings, and admitted that though predestination did not invariably damage religion, controversy about it did (III, 230; V, 90).

Wesley judged Socinians, the forerunners of Unitarian belief, "to be far worse than even a Predestinarian" (VIII, 13; VII, 27-28). He held Deists, who in their dedication to reason denied the supernatural and miraculous, to be as destructive of Christianity as Popery or immorality (II, 30, 313; VII, 265). "To convert a thousand Deists" by giving up the righteousness of God and the doctrine of justification, he argues, "is little more than it would be to convert as many Jews by allowing the Messiah is not yet come" (III, 345). Antinomians, who believed that faith exempted them from the demands of the law and freed them to indulge in any practice, drew Wesley's heavy fire. In his judgment, their pernicious doctrine is "still the main flood in England" (VI, 133).

Finally, Wesley was much more desirous of keeping Methodists sound in the faith than he was of correcting the faith of others. In several ways he set standards for their belief. As a leader of firm conviction, he published a collection of tracts entitled, *A Preservative Against Unsettled Notions in Religion,* and aimed it at the young preachers and at "all that can understand it." He tells a correspondent, this collection, "by the blessing of God, may help you from being tossed about with divers winds of doctrine" (IV, 272). He also inaugurated and for years continued to edit the *Arminian Magazine,* a journal expressly intended to promote his religious convictions and those of the Revival (VI, 283-84, 312ff.).

It was Wesley's hope that after his death Methodists would continue to "preach the old Methodist doctrines" (V, 143ff.). What these doctrines were he specified early in the Revival: "Our main doctrines, which include all the rest, are three—that of Repentance, of Faith and of Holiness" (II, 268). Somewhat later he emphasizes again our "three grand scriptural doctrines—Original Sin, Justification by Faith, and Holiness consequent thereon" (IV, 146). Elsewhere he calls these three doctrines "essential." After Whitefield's death in 1770, Wesley writes, "The grand, fundamental doctrines which Mr. Whitefield everywhere preached were those of the New Birth and Justification by Faith" (V, 224-25). A correspondent protested that the items in Whitefield's Calvinism were fundamental, but for Wesley they remained but opinions.

In his further concern for doctrinal standards, Wesley exhorted the preachers in America, "Let all of you be delivered to abide by the Methodist doctrine and discipline published in the four volumes of *Sermons* and the *Notes Upon the New Testament,* together with the *Large Minutes of the Conference*" (VII, 191). When asked to allow his people to choose leaders and stewards, he responds, "I have been uniform both in doctrine and discipline for above these fifty years; and it is a little too late for me to turn into a new path now I am grey-headed" (VIII, 196). Two or three of his preachers, he once admitted, did not think as they ought, but he says, "of them I have heard of no heresy which they preached; only a little smooth, undigested nonsense" (II, 93).

Wesley seemed fully in earnest about an orthodoxy that lies beyond mere opinion. But after years of service, he conceded that learned opinions are not half so helpful or destructive as he had thought when he was thirty (VIII, 271). He knew that ideas and correct beliefs do not save—only God does—and that where there is some error or ignorance, salvation may still come when "the main of what is preached is the truth as it is in Jesus; for it is only the gospel of Jesus Christ which is the power of God unto salvation" (II, 135). His generous spirit is further evident in this excerpt from one of his letters: "Touching the charity due those who are in error, I suppose we both likewise agree that really invincible ignorance never did nor ever shall exclude any man from heaven; and hence I doubt not but God will receive thousands of those who differ from me, even where I hold the truth" (II, 69; III, 203). For him, Christian love is the greatest prize of all as he characteristically witnesses in the close of a letter to Thomas Church: "That God may lead us both into all truth, and that we may not drop our love in the pursuit of it, is the continued prayer of, reverend Sir, Your friend and servant for Christ's sake, John Wesley" (II, 276).

John Wesley, Defender of the Faith! Only occasionally has Methodism paid such tribute to its founder. Some explanation for this neglect we have found in Wesley's dislike for controversy, though he engaged in it frequently; in his disregard for "mere opinions" in religion; and in his stress on the disposition of the heart as central to Christian faith and life. But we also noticed that he placed marked stress on fundamental doctrines, linked them to the Bible and to Christian tradition, and defended them against the distortions he perceived in others. Finally, we saw considerable evidence of his preoccupation with standards for Methodist belief and of his efforts to conform his people to them.

Perhaps the evidence of Wesley's commitment to orthodoxy got lost in his many broad concerns, his wide-ranging activities in the Revival, and in his extensive writings. Even so, the fact that Wesley was a man of firm commitment to the evangelical realities of the gospel, and that he encouraged others in the same commitment, seems well supported by his *Letters*.

9
The Confirmation of the Gospel

In New Testament times, it was comparatively easy to tell the Christians from the pagans. Paul knew, as did Wesley, that lives are changed when Christian reality is present. Both believed that the members of the community of Christ bear the marks of the one who calls them into its fellowship. Thus, in the New Testament as in the Wesleyan Revival, Christian faith was expected to make a significant, discernible difference in human lives, and often it did.

Both Paul and Wesley defended Christian truth and resisted its dilution and distortion. But they regarded truth, understood as proper belief, as an aid to living faith, not as a substitute for it. As they saw it, their task was to save souls and encourage them in righteous living. As a consequence, they were unwilling to allow people to rest content in the form without the power of godliness.

Both men insisted that as believers come to share in a new reality, they display the graces of a changed life. Some of these graces or evidences accompanied both men, taking the form of ecstatic manifestations. On occasion, they were compelled to question these extraordinary manifestations and to reckon with their abuse. But neither was prepared to give up likely signs of the Spirit's activity, simply because they were different or difficult to account for; neither afforded them undue significance, yet neither allowed them to be hurriedly dismissed.

We are now brought face to face with a vital issue. Is the claim of the Christian faith to transform life false? Are its promises empty? Are the converted merely deluded? Are the consequences of the Spirit's work discernible? Are charismatic displays fraudulent? Is encouragement in spiritual growth futile? In short, we are confronted by a perennial problem of the faith, one that is central to its existence: Is the gospel reality or is it illusion?

Wesley was fully aware of the importance of this problem and spared no effort in his life, thought, and work to resolve it. It was the gnawing problem of his own inner being until it was settled at Aldersgate. Thereafter, he was passionately concerned to assist others in solving this problem and finding a new life and a confident witness to its reality.

Throughout Wesley's *Letters* we find this pervasive concern for the reality of redemption. They contain several examples of his unflagging efforts to uphold the authenticity of the gospel: (1) his portrait of the character of those grasped by the gospel; (2) his belief in the assurance of the Spirit's activity and his acceptance of its unusual manifestations; (3) his dispute with those who desired to reduce the miraculous accompaniments of the Revival to mere enthusiasm; and (4) his extensive spiritual counseling by correspondence and pastoral service.

In Wesley's day, many saw and heard and yet doubted the reality of the Spirit's work, and our responses may be much the same as theirs. But at least we can attempt to show where Wesley stood on this critical issue and why, and review the evidence he presented to sustain his position.

Let us begin our examination of Wesley's belief that redemption is a reality that transforms human lives by picking up a theme we discussed in the previous chapter. Belief or "opinion," in his judgment, does not save, even if it is properly orthodox. The point is finely made in his comment on a book that he had just read. "If anything is wanting," in Mr. Jones' book on the doctrine of the trinity, Wesley asserts, "it is the application, lest it should appear to be a merely speculative doctrine, which has no influence on our heart or lives" (VI, 213).

In some contexts then, Wesley seemed willing to call all theological statements mere "opinions," that is, intellectual constructs that in themselves possess no saving power. "A string of opinions is no more Christian faith," he declares, "than a string of beads is Christian holiness. It is not assent to any opinion or any number of opinions.

A man may assent to three or three-and-twenty creeds, he may assent to all the Old Testament and the New Testament (at least, as far as he understands them), and yet have no Christian faith at all" (II, 381).

In this important letter to Dr. Conyers Middleton, Wesley contends further that faith in redemptive reality is the power to see through the veil to things spiritual; it is the divine evidence or conviction of being reconciled to God. To believe, then, in the Christian sense, is "to walk in the light of eternity, and to have a clear sight of and confidence in the Most High reconciled to me through the Son of His love" (II, 382). Here he has not much changed an early statement in which he had affirmed, "I take religion to be . . . a constant ruling habit of soul, a renewal of our minds in the image of God, a recovery of the divine likeness, a still-increasing conformity of heart and life to the pattern of our most holy Redeemer" (I, 152).

In the same letter to Dr. Middleton, Wesley gives us a "plain, naked portraiture of a Christian." He is one who is abased before God, continually dependent on him, with the firmest confidence in him. He is conformed in the image of love to all people and displays right affections. He is artless in a sincerity that produces right actions free of pride, free of censure, and happy in God that he is loved by Him. To this portrayal, Wesley believed, the character of a Methodist should conform. Christianity, he concludes, "is that system of doctrine . . . which promises it shall be mine (provided I will not rest 'till I attain), and which tells me how I may attain it" (II, 380).

Wesley contended valiantly for the reality of the gospel's power to renew broken lives and to make them whole. He desired all to have a firm grasp of gospel truth, but he desired even more its confirmation in the hearts and lives of his people. His apostolic purpose was to assist the translation of the promises of the gospel into

110

actuality in human lives. He seems dissatisfied with anything less.

One pervasive mark of the reality of redemption—of Christian character—Wesley maintained was the witness of the Spirit to this work and character. When the gospel is effective, the resulting changes in people are sufficiently evident to be noticed. Those renewed by the Spirit's power will receive an "assurance" of its redeeming activity (II, 64). Thus, he laid great stress on the doctrine of assurance, or the witness of the Spirit. In the first year of the Revival he affirms, "I believe that every Christian who has not yet received it should pray for the witness of God's Spirit with his spirit that he is a child of God" (I, 274).

When faith is redemptively operative, it will produce not only pardon in justification but also renewal in regeneration. The Spirit will make a "manifestation" or an "inner impression on the soul" of the believer; it will convey a "discovery" or "deep sense" of the reality of grace, Wesley contends. Of these evidences of grace he affirms, "Whoever has these, inwardly feels them; and if he understands his Bible, he discerns from whence they come. Observe, what he inwardly feels is these fruits themselves; whence they come he learns from the Bible. This is my doctrine concerning inward feelings, and has been for above these forty years" (V, 363).

Wesley was aware that there is great variation in the Spirit's work. Sometimes it is overwhelming in its power; sometimes it is gentle, almost invisible, in its manner (VII, 298). He warns that "There is a danger of every believer's mistaking the voice of the enemy or of their own imagination for the voice of God. And you can distinguish one from the other, not by any written rule, but only by *the unction of the Holy One*" (V, 241). He discovered, too, in his own life and in the life of his people, the necessity of qualifying his doctrine of assurance. In 1747, in a letter to his brother Charles, he tempered the

111

exacting demands of his earlier statements. In 1768 he writes to another, "I have not for many years thought a consciousness of acceptance to be essential to justifying faith" (V, 359). In unusual cases, he concludes, some Christians may not receive an assurance of their state of grace (V, 50, 358; VI, 88, 323). Despite these second thoughts, he did not drop the doctrine but continued to urge every Christian to seek assurance, not as a necessity but as a "common privilege" (V, 359; VII, 61).

Wesley's theological conviction and his personal and pastoral experience did not allow him to equate assurance with final perseverance. The witness of the Spirit, he believed, was not a permanent possession that endured through life and accompanied one into eternity (I, 256, 290, 308; III, 305). It could be given or withdrawn, depending on the faithfulness of the believer or the unfathomable designs of God (II, 89, 103, 138). Though it endured moment by moment and was subject to variation, for most people it was the normal accompaniment of their relationship to God.

Wesley's father, on his deathbed in 1748, wrote to his son, "The inward witness, son, the inward witness, that is the proof, the strongest proof, of Christianity" (II, 135). But Wesley needed no reminder of this truth. It had been his since his heart was "strangely warmed" at Aldersgate. Through the years he had made accommodations in the doctrine of assurance in the light of his experience. But he never surrendered his conviction that the reality of redemption could be discerned both in its fruits and in the testimony of the Spirit in the hearts of believers. For him, redemption was reality, it was not illusion.

Though Wesley was convinced of the reality of renewal in Christ and of the confident assurance of renewal bestowed by the Spirit, many of his contemporaries were not. He lived in the age of reason, when people looked askance at peculiar manifestations and emotional dis-

112

plays. The devotees of reason had strong supporters in the Christian church as well as among those more worldly. They were alarmed by the many manifestations of the Spirit's activity in the Revival and by the expectation that such experiences were the right of every Christian. They were certain that these "evidences" of the Spirit's work were in fact pretension and delusion, if not deception altogether. In a word, these manifestations were not reality but illusion; the Revival was infected by that most unseemly of sins—enthusiasm.

Wesley was keenly aware that he was laying himself open to such charges. His comments on the publication of his *Journal* accounts of the early years of the Revival betray his uneasiness:

I considered deeply with myself what I ought to do—whether to declare the things I had seen or not. I consulted the most serious friends I had. They all agreed I ought to declare them; that the work itself was of such a kind as ought in nowise to be concealed; and, indeed, that the unusual circumstances now attending it made it impossible that it should. . . . This very difficulty occurred: "Will not my speaking of this be boasting? at least, will it not be accounted so?" They replied: "If you speak of it as your own work, it will be vanity and boasting all over; but if you ascribe it wholly to God, if you give Him all the praise, it will not. And if, after this, some will account it so still, you must be content and bear the burthen." . . . I yielded, and transcribed my papers for the press; only labouring as far as possible to "render unto God the things which are God's," and to give Him the praise of His own work (II, 264-65).

And his fears were well founded.

He was charged with enthusiasm for announcing that God was "working a great and extraordinary work

113

in the earth" among the people called Methodists (II, 262). Such talk, his opponents said, was both arrogance and blasphemy. Wesley counters in these words, "I do talk of such a work. But I deny the consequence; for if God has begun a great work, then the saying He has is no enthusiasm" (III, 270). In support of his belief he listed the conformity of the Revival to Scripture and reason, the many conversions attended by the Spirit, and the rapid advance of the Revival (II, 263).

His critics accused him of pretending to "an inward light as a private guide and director," thereby placing himself above the written Word (IV, 123). This accusation he flatly denied: "I have declared again and again that I make the Word of God the rule of all my actions, and that I no more follow any secret impulse instead thereof than I follow Mahomet or Confucius" (II, 205). He refused to make any claim for particular, immediate inspiration, or to an apostle's power to work signs and wonders. All Wesley claimed was that God used him to help in the conversion of sinners.

Church leaders denounced as enthusiasm his many references to the work of a particular providence that led him to see God's hand in all things, bringing good from evil, and spreading the Revival (II, 208). Yet he held to God's providential care as the life blood of his faith. He laments, "The doctrine of a Particular Providence is what exceeding few persons understand—at least, not practically, so as to apply it to every circumstance of life. This I want, to see God acting in everything, and disposing all for His own glory and His creatures' good" (III, 139).

Many leaders within the established church, as well as many deists without, were suspicious of the conversions that prevailed in the Revival. They were offended by the emotional "excesses" of Wesley's listeners and by their joyful witness to the work of the Spirit. At first, even George Whitefield was disturbed by the unusual signs that accompanied Wesley's preaching. Having said as much to Wesley, he experienced extraordinary manifestations in response to his own preaching the very next day (I, 330). Though Wesley did not require or encourage charismatic displays, he did not discount them either. He expected dramatic things to happen in the course of the Spirit's work.

His detractors viewed conversion itself with misgivings. One of them charged that, even if Wesley did not, "Your followers, however, do pretend to the grace of miraculous conversion." To which Wesley responds, "Is there any conversion that is not miraculous? Is conversion a natural or supernatural work?" (IV, 40). Though he laid no claim to the performance of miracles, he was forced to believe that God works in conversion in powerful and arresting ways. He writes, "I acknowledge that I have seen with my eyes and heard with my ears several things which, to the best of my judgement cannot be accounted for by the ordinary course of natural causes, and which I therefore believe ought to be 'ascribed to the extraordinary interposition of God.'" Then he addresses the point at issue: "If any man choose to style these miracles, I reclaim not. I have diligently inquired into the facts. I have weighed the preceding and following circumstances. I have strove to account for them in a natural way. I could not without doing violence to my reason" (II, 256, 317ff.).

And, of course, Wesley's critics took the doctrine of assurance and the testimony to it by many of his followers to be conclusive proof of enthusiasm. Within his own family, his brother Samuel was concerned about Wesley's insistence on the witness of the Spirit, and the probability that it would lead to enthusiasm (I, 290, 308). Others were sure that the worst had happened. Wesley's extended correspondence with "John Smith" was devoted primarily to this theme. Wesley's anonymous opponent argued for an assurance that was reasonable and therefore indisputable (II, 103 *passim*). But Wesley believed that assurance was granted by the Spirit through faith and could not be known or demonstrated in the way that "John Smith" desired. For Wesley, assurance was rooted in the regeneration of a sinful life by the Spirit; for many of his clerical opponents, regeneration was not a viable reality, or, in Wesley's view, it was sadly misunderstood.

Many of his critics, not satisfied with what they saw and heard, demanded some sign of the divine origin and power of the Revival. "Show us a sign and we will believe," they pleaded. "What will you believe?" asks Wesley. "I hope no more than is written in the Book of God. And thus far you might venture to believe, even without a miracle" (II, 262). Again, he complains that the "unreasonableness of the common demand to prove our doctrine by miracles" not only subverts Scripture, it also fails to understand human nature (II, 105). If men were granted great and powerful signs, he argues, "all this would not force them to believe; but many would still stand just where they did before, seeing men may 'harden their hearts,' against miracles as well as against arguments" (II, 258). He said that if miracles have the power to convince, present doubters ought rather to be firm believers, for what is more a miracle than the conversion of a sinner? And this occurs on every hand (II, 136). Thus Wesley brought his case to its summation.

Illusion does not produce beneficent results. Unshaken in this conviction, Wesley was willing to rest his case for the reality of the Revival on its consequences. He invited those who had doubts about it to go and talk to people, examine their beliefs and practices, visit the towns that had experienced some changes, and to draw their own conclusions. He challenged Thomas Church to compare the results of his respective doctrines and preaching with those of Wesley's to see who had changed sinners into upright walkers (II, 200-201). The confirmation of the Revival, Wesley maintained, was to be found in the confirmation of the gospel in the lives that had been transformed by it. Wesley clung tenaciously to this experimental test to validate his "practical, experimental" religion.

He documents his case in a letter to Dr. Gibson, Bishop of London, by presenting an impressive "cloud of witnesses": "The habitual drunkard that was is now temperate in all things; the whoremonger now flees fornication; he that stole, steals no more, but works with his hands; he that cursed or swore, perhaps in every sentence, has now learned to serve the Lord with fear and rejoice unto Him with reverence; those formerly enslaved to various habits of sin are now brought to uniform habits of holiness. These are demonstrable facts: I can name the men, with their places of abode" (II, 290).

Wesley's battle against charges of enthusiasm, of presumed illusion in the Revival, derived from his foremost responsibility: the confirmation of the reality of the gospel in the lives of his people. He understood his duties to include the personal care of the souls entrusted to his keeping. He took time out from his busy rounds to visit, by going from house to house, the members of many of his societies and insisted, not always successfully, that his preachers do the same (I, 204-5; II, 11). With solicitous vigilance he carried out the responsibilities of discipline, purging the societies of those who did not walk upright before the Lord (I, 352; V, 204). Without ceasing, by word and practice, he urged his people to employ all the means of grace: prayer; searching the Scriptures; taking the Lord's Supper at every opportunity; fasting; and attending preaching services and the meetings of the societies and classes (I, 66; II, 202-3; IV, 272; VI, 201).

To these many pastoral duties Wesley added one more: he carried on a voluminous correspondence with persons in need of pastoral care. Through this correspondence he also endeavored to be a shepherd to his flock. In many letters he advanced spiritual counsel on a wide range of practical problems that beset his people. To one suffering bereavement, he offered consolation and encouragement (II, 144). To one afflicted by sickness, he suggested using the time of illness to spiritual advantage (VI, 278). To one wounded by chastisement at the hands of others, he extended understanding and support (II, 150ff.) To one lax in the duties of parenthood, he sent a stern rebuke (VI, 148f.). To one inclined to gossip, he made clear the dangers of unkindness and hypocrisy (V, 324). His concerns encompassed all the problems of life that hindered growth in grace.

Many of his letters were directed to his preachers and dealt with their perplexities and temptations. He wrote a firm letter to one preacher, tempted to give up his calling, and admonished him to stand fast (V, 292). He addressed comforting words to a new preacher who was uneasy about his vocation (II, 84). He instructed many of his assistants in the manner and purpose of their preaching (III, 34, 84). He chastised those who neglected discipline (VI, 185), or failed to care for their members (II, 11), or insisted on staying too long in one place (VI, 49), or quarreled with other ministers (IV, 192ff.), or refused to accept his directions (IV, 375), or engaged too much in controversy (IV, 209ff.; VIII, 150). The faithfulness of his preachers to the gospel was important, Wesley believed, not only for their souls but also for the souls of those whom they served.

Wesley wrote hundreds of letters to persons who found the life of faith difficult and at times discouraging. Characteristically, these letters analyzed their recipients' problems, offered them advice, and ended with an encouragement to continue in the pursuit of faith and righteousness. This letter is typical: "Do you still find a witness in yourself that God has purified your heart from sin? Do you never feel any return of pride, or anger, or self-will, or foolish desire? Do you steadily endure, seeing Him that is invisible? Are you always sensible of His loving presence? Are you constantly happy in Him? Does He keep you sleeping and waking, and make your very dream devout? O stand fast in glorious liberty" (V, 45; VIII, 279)! Another letter defines a problem more precisely: "The great danger which I apprehend you to be in is that of healing your hurt slightly. It is God that has wounded you; and let Him heal the soul which hath sinned against Him. O beware that you never rest, or desire any rest, till Christ is revealed in your heart" (II, 172).

In yet another letter the counsel is even more sharply pointed: "Beware of your own spirit! You bite like a bulldog; when you seize, you never let go" (VI, 141). Another time Wesley offers this sage advice: "Do you labour to get your own living, abhorring idleness as you abhor hell-fire? The devil tempts other men; but an idle man's brain is the devil's shop where he is continually working mischief" (III, 12). In a typical letter of correction, he concludes in a gentler spirit, "The Lord God enlighten the eyes of your understanding and soften and enlarge your heart" (III, 192)!

These letters are but a small sample of the many Wesley wrote to admonish, advise, and encourage his people. He made their problems and difficulties his own and as much as he could, he sought faithfully to enhance the reality of redemption in their lives.

Throughout his years of service to God, Wesley exercised great concern for the effective realization of the gospel. He emphasized the dimensions of character as a result of being born anew. He encouraged his people in their confidence that through faith they had become children of God. He resisted his critics' charges of enthusiasm in his support of the evidences of the Spirit's power. And with sensitivity and expectation he counseled those who sought to enter into the fullness of the Christian life. In steadfast faith he held to the gospel's promise of a power of godliness that went beyond mere form. As an apostle called to shepherd his people, he felt he could do no less.

10
The Practice of Christianity

Christianity is a religion of love. Just as Paul and Wesley believed that the preference for opinion over fundamental truth subverted Christianity, so they believed that undue preoccupation with spectacular manifestations of the Spirit's presence did likewise. Both held that correct beliefs as well as tongues and prophecy must give way to active love. They held that faith must give rise to works, and while humans are not saved by works, neither are they saved without them. For both men, the commitment of faith had implications for the whole of life.

Many of the converts of Paul and Wesley were tempted to compromise the gospel and to depart from its teachings. Too often they were beguiled into thinking that faith ended with the nurture of their own souls. But they found little support in Paul (nor did they in Wesley) for this supposition. Both men exhorted their converts to press on to their high calling in Christ and to fulfill the great commandment of love to neighbor. Paul and Wesley did not spare any effort to assist believers to show forth the fruits of the Spirit.

Paul's New Testament epistles exhibit a common pattern. The apostle first probed various aspects of the Christian gospel, then he applied what he had said to the lives of Christ's followers. He joined the two parts of his letters with the decisive word "therefore." Because of what God through Christ did for us, therefore, in gratitude we turn to the service of others. For him, this single word linked Christian faith to Christian practice. It marked the transition from belief to morality and underscored the important truth that practice derives from living faith.

Wesley, too, could not stress the "practical application" of the gospel too much. But in doing so neither he nor Paul thought to subordinate redemptive reality to the demands of practical living. Both were convinced that love and service flowed naturally and inescapably from lives that had been transformed by the Spirit.

The last problem that we want to examine then is

the problem of "faith and works." In one sense it is the last problem of the Christian faith, though in another sense it is also its first problem. In other words, to consider fully the practical consequences of the gospel, we have to go back and consider its foundation and dynamics.

Are we in such bondage to sin that we require help from outside? If we on our own cannot perform works pleasing to God, can we do anything to obtain saving faith? Should duty guide our actions, or should they spring from renewed desire? Are the demands for maturity in love so high as to be impossible and destructive of selfless simplicity? Does Christian conscience have anything distinctive to say in the realm of public affairs? Does our eternal destiny hinge on what we are, what we believe, or what we do?

Wesley's *Letters* shed some light on some of these problems. Four aspects of how he deals with the issue of faith and works merit investigation: (1) Wesley's conviction that all are fallen and unable to produce faith or to do good; (2) his insistence that faith is both the gift and work of God and also a human responsibility; (3) his encouragement of believers to expect to be made perfect in love; and (4) his dedication to works of love in response to the needs of a disordered world.

The bondage of sin is the chief problem of Christian practice. Wesley maintained that the work of sin is to produce still more sin, and that its power must be broken before the works of God's creatures become pleasing to Him. Wesley is certain that this creature of God, "this silly, laughing, trifling animal," is born for eternity (V, 336). Yet he confesses, "I cannot admire either the wisdom or virtue or happiness of mankind. Wherever I have been, I have found the bulk of mankind, Christian as well as heathen, deplorably ignorant, vicious, and miserable. . . . Sin and pain are on every side. And who can account for this but on the supposition that we are in a fallen state" (VI, 61-62). He repeats the theme: "I have declared a thousand times there is no goodness in man till he is justified; no merit either before or after" (V, 270). He drives it home in a strong admonition to his sister: "Surely, whenever your eyes are opened, whenever you see your own tempers, with the advantages you have enjoyed, you will make no scruple to pronounce yourself (whores and murderers not excepted) the very chief of sinners" (II, 14).

As a consequence of the universal blight of sin, human nature is rendered helpless and can be brought to life only in a New Birth (I, 328; II, 71ff.). In a brief letter to John Fletcher in 1771, Wesley sums up his convictions about the bondage of sin: "I always did for between these thirty and forty years clearly assert the total fall of man and his utter inability to do any good of himself; the absolute necessity of the grace and Spirit of God to raise even a good thought or desire in our hearts; the Lord's rewarding no work and accepting of none but so far as they proceed from his preventing, convincing, and converting grace through the Beloved; the blood and righteousness of Christ being the sole meritorious cause of our salvation. Who is there in England that has asserted these things more strongly and steadily than I have done" (V. 231)?

To produce good works, Wesley insists, a person must first be renewed by the Holy Spirit: "I deny the necessity, nay possibility of good works as previous to this salvation; as previous to faith, or those fruits of faith, 'righteousness and peace and joy in the Holy Ghost.'" And to make sure he is not misunderstood, he adds, "This is my real sentiment, not a slip of my pen, neither any proof of my want of accuracy" (II, 190-91).

Perhaps we should add, and it is fair to Wesley's understanding, that the "good" works of the unregenerate could add to the store of good in the world and help offset the vast store of evil. But these works are not "good" for the one who does them. They are tinged with self-regard and self-seeking, and often they involve the use and manipulation of others; frequently, too, they seek to earn God's favor, that is, to manipulate God. Therefore, the first thing to be noted in Wesley's view of faith and works is his insistence that good works flow only from the person who has first entered into goodness through faith in God.

It follows then from Wesley's logic and experience that the work of faith is God's work. In fact, this is precisely what he professes: "Saving faith is both the gift and the work of God" (IV, 212). Faith is not a work that the unsaved can perform for their salvation; their bondage in sin makes the act of faith impossible for them (I, 239-40; IV, 331). To make certain that his affirmation that faith, and the justification before God that accompanies it, was not misunderstood, he asserts: "I think on Justification just as I have done any time these seven-and-twenty years, and just as Mr. Calvin does." That is, the initial act of faith rests in God's hands. And he adds, "I do not differ from him an hair's breadth" (IV, 298). But to affirm that faith is the gift and work of God raises a critical problem. If the unregenerate are caught in the bondage of sin, and faith, which they cannot will, is their only escape, what can they do to be saved?

Wesley complicated the problem when he added to his conviction that faith is the gift and work of God another firm conviction: to be saved one had to believe. In a critical passage Wesley attempts to solve the problem: "Undoubtedly faith is *the work of God;* and yet it is *the duty of man* to believe. And every man may believe *if* he will, though not *when* he will. If he seek faith in the appointed ways, sooner or later the power of the Lord will be present, whereby (1) God works, and by *His* power (2) man believes. In order of thinking God's working goes first; but not in order of time. Believing is the act of the human mind, strengthened by the power of God" (VII, 202-3).

But even here Wesley seemed intent on having it both ways: faith is from God, yet man believes in the power of God. Was he simply confused and, therefore, asserted contradictions? Or did he accurately reflect a reality in Christian thought and experience that eludes rational explanation and rests in the mysteries of God?

In a broader setting, the problem is exemplified in Wesley's strife with the Moravians and the Calvinists. The Moravians held to a doctrine of stillness that enjoined complete passivity before God and abstention from all means of grace. They believed man had no part in faith except to wait quietly for its bestowal by the Spirit. Despite the help Wesley had received from the Moravians, once he understood the full implications of their doctrine, he broke relations with them (I, 345ff.; II, 80ff.; III, 52ff.). In Wesley's judgment the Calvinists also exposed their followers to this sort of Antinomian peril. They held that, as a predestined gift, faith was bestowed on some and withheld from others, entirely apart from the desire or effort of either (IV, 331; VIII, 95).

Both Moravians and Calvinists accused Wesley of promoting salvation by works, and perhaps with some reason. They remembered that he had argued that faith is a condition performed by man. If not by man, "by whom then?" he had asked. "God gives me the power to believe. But does He believe for me? He works faith in me. But still it is not I that believe? And if so, is not believing an inward act performed by me" (IV, 220)? Still Wesley protested that he did not hold salvation by works. "None of us talk of being accepted for our works" he insists. "That is the Calvinist slander. But we all maintain we are not saved without works, that works are a condition (though not the meritorious cause) of final salvation." (Here Wesley assumes a distinction between salvation in this life and in the next—final salvation.) He adds, "It is by faith in the righteousness and blood of Christ that we are enabled to do all good works; and it is for the sake of these that all who fear God and work righteousness are accepted by Him" (VI, 76-77). Works are important, indeed vital, but for Wesley they followed, and did not replace, faith.

Wesley himself was charged with Calvinism because of his insistence on the priority of faith and its full dependence on God's grace. He had once written, "None are or can be saved but those who are by faith made inwardly and outwardly holy. But this holy faith is the gift of God; and He is never straitened for time. He can as easily give this faith in a moment as in a thousand years. He frequently does give it on a death-bed, in answer to the prayer of believers, but rarely if ever to those who had continued unholy upon the presumption that He would save them *at last*" (V, 337-38; IV, 331). From this and similar statements many enlightened clergy in the Church and most deists concluded that works had little place in Wesley's thought and proceeded to lump him together with the Calvinists and Moravians.

Thus Wesley managed to draw fire from both sides. He was charged with disparaging works by some and with trusting in them for salvation by others. That he was belabored by these two opposing parties may suggest that he was somewhere near the truth.

Those who lived in the power of faith led changed lives, Wesley believed. Through faith they were brought to a New Birth; they were freed from the guilt of sin; they found that the power of sin was broken (VI, 217). In this process of regeneration they became new creatures in Christ. Wesley describes this New Birth in these words: "It is that great change which God works in the soul when He brings it into life; when He raises it from the death of sin to the life of righteousness. It is the change wrought in the whole soul by the almighty Spirit of God, when it is 'created anew in Christ Jesus,' when it is 'renewed after the image of God in righteousness and true holiness'; when the love of the world is changed into the love of God, pride into humility, passion into meekness, hatred, envy, malice, into a sincere, tender, disinterested love to all mankind. In a word, it is that change whereby the 'earthly, sensual, devilish' mind is turned into 'the mind which was in Christ Jesus' " (IV, 382-83).

Persons thus reborn exhibited the "fruits of the Spirit." And the choicest fruit, to which Wesley devoted much attention, was Christian perfection—being made perfect in love (III, 221; IV, 10, 71-72). "You have only one thing to do," he observes, "leaving the first principles of the doctrine of Christ, go on to perfection" (VII, 322). "This doctrine," he stresses, "is the grand depositum which God has lodged with the people called Methodists; and for the sake of propagating this chiefly He appeared to have raised us up" (VIII, 238). Perfection is the fulfillment of the work of grace begun in the New Birth. It should be the end of all the Christian's seeking: "Entire sanctification, or Christian perfection, is neither more nor less than pure love—love expelling sin and governing both the heart and life of a child of God. The Refiner's fire purges out all that is contrary to love, and that many times by a pleasing smart" (V, 223). Or put somewhat differently: "Perfect love and Christian liberty are the very same thing; and those two expressions are equally proper, being equally scriptural" (V, 203).

From the beginning to the end of his life Wesley pursued the life of holiness and sought to be made perfect in love. After his evangelical awakening, however, he came to a new realization of the means by which such love is attained. He believed no longer that love was the result of prayer and devotion and works of righteousness. Rather he was convinced that, like justification and the New Birth, Christian perfection, too, was a gift of grace bestowed through faith by the Holy Spirit (IV, 376; VII, 222, 267; VIII, 190). It was not a state that human effort could attain; it was a fruit of the Spirit's activity.

Since by their own efforts people could not attain

perfection, Wesley encouraged them to hope and pray and live for its coming. He was aware of the dangers of stressing the gift of perfect love. He admits that to define its requirements too rigorously "is to sap the foundations of it and to destroy it from the face of the earth. I am jealous over you," he assures his reader, "I am afraid lest, by grasping at a shadow, you should have let go the substance—lest, by aiming at a perfection which we cannot have till hereafter, you should cast away that which now belongs to the children of God" (IV, 251; VI, 88). Similarly he acknowledges in debate with one who disagreed with him, "If I set the mark too high, I drive men into needless fears; if you set it too low, you drive them into hell-fire" (III, 168).

Wesley proposed to do neither one nor the other, and his success may be judged by these words: "They that love God with all their heart and all men as themselves are scripturally perfect. And surely such there are; otherwise the promise of God would be a mere mockery of human weakness. Hold fast this. But then remember, on the other hand, you have this treasure in an earthen vessel; you dwell in a poor, shattered house of clay, which presses down the immortal spirit. Hence all your thoughts, words, and actions are so imperfect, so far from coming up to the standard (that law of love, which, but for the corruptible body, your soul would answer in all instances), that you may well say till you go to Him you love:

> Every moment, Lord, I need
> The merit of thy death" (IV, 208).

Nevertheless, a number of his people were distressed by their lack of perfect love, and Wesley addressed many of his letters to their problems (IV, 20, 252, 260, 300; V, 291, 216; VI, 59, 138, 238, etc.). Some he cautions, in the words of Fénelon, that "simplicity is that grace which frees the soul from all unnecessary reflections upon itself" (V, 193). But he never relinquished his commit-

129

ment to perfection as the privilege of believers, even though several of his letters to Charles disclose that he considered doing so (V, 88, 314). "The most prevailing fault among the Methodists," he laments with unerring judgment, "is to be *too outward* in religion. We are continually forgetting that the kingdom of God is *within us,* and that our fundamental principle is, We are saved by *faith,* producing all *inward* holiness, not by works, by any externals whatsoever" (V, 289).

In making perfect love the guiding principle of Christian perfection, Wesley again set a goal that far exceeded human resolve and effort to attain it. In his understanding, Christian practice aimed at works of love, at a purity of intention and quality of action that truly fit God's creatures to be His children. He believed that the gift of faith secured the gift of love and that all things are possible for love. His *Letters* clearly demonstrate that he never disregarded or discouraged works produced by love. Quite the reverse. Without ceasing, he contended for works perfected in love, but he did so in full awareness that his lofty demands could be met only by faithful believers empowered by the Spirit both to will and to do.

The practice of Christianity is the practice of love and, as Wesley saw it, love is to be applied over the whole range of human existence. He conceives religion "to be no other than love; the love of God and of all mankind. . . . This love we believe to be the medicine of life, the never-failing remedy for all the evils of a disordered world, for all the miseries and vices of men." He longs to see the religion of love "established in the world," where it will show "itself by its fruits; continually springing forth, not only in all innocence (for love worketh no ill to his neighbour), but likewise in every kind of beneficence, spreading virtue and happiness all around it" (II, 270).

Yet this inclusive concern for all mankind does not rule out the Christian's particular affection for some: "This universal benevolence does in no wise interfere with a

130

peculiar regard for his relations, friends, and benefactors, a fervent love for his country, and the most endeared affection to all men of integrity, of clear and generous virtue" (II, 377). More specifically, Wesley desires "a league offensive and defensive with every soldier of Christ" (IV, 218, 236ff.; V, 143-44). No matter how widely they may differ from us, he affirms, all who follow after "holiness of heart and life" are my "brother and sister and mother" (VI, 61; IV, 143).

He encouraged all to be "social, open, active, Christians." The love of the Christian, he avows, "is in itself generous and disinterested; springing from no view of advantage to himself, from no regard to profit or praise— no, not even the pleasure of loving. This is the daughter, not the parent, of affection. By experience he knows that social love, if it mean the love of our neighbour, is absolutely different from self-love, even of the most allowable kind—just as different as the objects at which they point. And yet it is sure that, if they are under due regulations, each will give additional force to the other till they mix together never to be divided" (II, 377).

The "social love" of the Christian entailed important social obligations in Wesley's view; their list is impressive, especially in light of the practices of the time. A number of pioneering social services were instituted by Wesley and his people in response to the pressing needs all around them; several are detailed in Wesley's significant letter to Vincent Perronet. Wesley was assisted in providing medical service to persons "ill of chronic disorders." His societies made temporary provision for some who lacked other support, chiefly feeble and aged widows. He sponsored an experimental school for "near sixty children" who were taught to read, write, and figure and were instructed in the "sound principles of religion." He established a loan fund from which distressed Methodists could borrow on repayment within three months (II, 292-311).

He was appalled at the state of the prisons in England, visited their prisoners and, with some success, urged responsible authorities to improve the conditions of these institutions (IV, 127-28). He tried to improve the lot of French prisoners taken in the war with England (IV, 73, 78). He accepted and supported "The Strangers' Friend Society" through which some of his societies aided those outside the Methodist circle: "poor strangers, having no parish, or friend at hand to help them" (VII, 308).

Much of Wesley's work was carried on among the downtrodden and dispossessed. He was all too well acquainted with the bitter poverty in which many of his people lived. He deplored the "scarcity of provisions" and an economy that permitted such want (V, 350ff.). "I love the poor," he said quite simply (III, 229). He stressed the importance of association with them and of winning them to Christ. To one woman who held herself apart from the poor, Wesley gives this assurance and instruction: "I have found some of the uneducated poor who have exquisite taste and sentiment; and many, very many of the rich who have scarcely any at all. . . . I want you to converse more, abundantly more, with the poorest of the people, who, if they have not taste, have souls, which you may forward on their way to heaven" (VI, 206).

Wesley was clear and decisive in his convictions about stewardship. "You are not the proprietor of anything," he reminds one of his flock. "Not of one shilling in the world. You are only a steward of what another entrusts you with, to be laid out not according to your will, but His" (III, 122). He berates reluctant givers, saying, "If the people were more alive to God, they would be more liberal. There is money enough" (VII, 247). His own practice of stewardship often has been noted. "Money never stays with *me,*" he testifies. "It would burn me if it did. I throw it out of my hands as soon as possible, lest it should find a way into my heart" (V, 108-9). This was no idle boast. Through the extraordinary sale of inexpensive literature that he prepared for his people, he easily could have become wealthy. But he gave his money away, and acknowledges toward the close of his life, "I have *two* silver teaspoons at *London*, and *two* at *Bristol*. This is all I have at present; and I shall not buy any more while so many around me want bread" (VI, 230).

Wesley also followed the dictates of love and justice into the realm of public affairs. He was interested in politics, aware of its complexities, and concerned for the state of the nation (V, 371; VI, 175-76). He detested war and was greatly disturbed over the events leading up to and the outbreak of the American War of Independence (VI, 150, 161, 168, etc.). He was a passionate advocate of religious liberty and vehemently protested the restraints imposed on Methodists. About one such instance of oppression he inquires scornfully, "where, then, is English liberty? the liberty of Christians? Yea, of every rational creature, who as such has a right to worship God according to his own conscience" (VIII, 231)?

He condemned the bribery of public officials and the buying of votes (IV, 107, 271). Repeatedly he deplored the widespread practice of smuggling. A few of his people were involved and he advises his preachers to "tear up this evil by the roots" (VI, 236). He denounced those who made and those who intemperately consumed spirituous liquors. His followers he advises to "touch no dram. It is liquid fire. It is a sure though slow poison. It saps the very springs of life" (V, 134). He was dead set against slavery and agitated for its abolition (VI, 126). The last letter he wrote was to William Wilberforce denouncing "that execrable villany" and encouraging him to persevere "till even American slavery (the vilest that ever saw the sun) shall vanish away" (VIII, 265).

Did John Wesley practice what he preached? Did he consistently relate faith and works to each other in his life, thought, and service? His *Letters* contain considerable evidence to support the conclusion that he did. He

133

firmly believed that the work of sin produces still more sin, and that humans need desperately to be delivered from their bondage. He found the way of forgiveness and renewal of life in God's work of faith in his needy creatures. He persistently enforced in believers the need for works of love of the highest quality. And he supported and engaged in works of righteousness in the service of the inhabitants of a stricken world. Thus did Wesley order and relate the work of sin, the work of faith, works of love, and works of righteousness.

All these realities are exemplified in Wesley's life. In his thought each reality had its place, and he effectively joined them together. In his service to God he solicited these realities and sustained them in the lives of the members of his societies. We conclude that Wesley was an apostle, come belatedly into the world, who in God's grace served honorably the cause of Scriptural Christianity.

A Letter to John Wesley

St. George
Staten Island, N.Y.
August 24, 1982

Dear Mr. Wesley,

Please allow me to share with you some thoughts that have occurred to me of late. Much to my benefit I have been studying the letters you have left behind. Impressively and consistently they exhibit concern for the many responsibilities that fell to you in your role in the Revival that now bears your name.

I have wondered about the implications of your apostleship for my generation. (Please allow me to use the term apostleship, even though it may cause you embarrassment.) Often I have tried to translate what I take to be the genuine marks of apostleship—the care and cure of souls—into language now in common use. Perhaps it will not be an undue burden if I attempt here to give contemporary expression to four primary themes I have found in your letters.

1. Is it not true that of all people an apostle is one who has been embraced by divine love? Is not his call an enabling call, together with a commission for service? Are not the breadth and depth of his apostolic activities the consequences of the power that has laid hold of him? I believe that you would answer each of these questions in the affirmative.

2. Again, I conclude that a first responsibility of an apostle is to support the truth of love against misunderstanding and distortion. Love is the truth of our inner being. It can easily be frustrated or denied by disputes about its truthfulness. Patiently, sympathetically, the apostle declines to accept our reasoned refutations of the truth of love. Perhaps this is one meaning of orthodoxy. It is the support of considered convictions that open rather than close the human heart to love's invasion.

3. Further, an apostle nurtures the reality of love once it has brought us under siege. The invasion of love exacts a painful price, requiring us to surrender some of our proud and cherished views of ourselves. Too easily we have settled

for approximations of love's reality. But since illusions do not heal, an apostle's duty is to assist both the self-satisfied and the struggling to go beyond the counterfeits of love to the reality of love itself.

4. Finally, through works of love and their encouragement in others, an apostle demonstrates that love touches and transforms all human activities and relationships. The practice of love is natural, even inevitable, for the beloved and loving person who shares love freely without thought of return. An apostle, therefore, wisely does not impose works apart from the gift of love. Tasks grow out of the gift and are gladly undertaken.

Unless I misread your letters, Mr. Wesley, yours was a most demanding and encompassing commission, with duties that clearly exceeded human powers. The work of an apostle rests wholly on the reality of divine love. As Paul, chief of the apostles, said, without love we are nothing. This is a hard truth for my age and for every age since Paul first stated it so graphically. May I assert my belief that you share this conviction, and that it contains the secret of your life and ministry?

I may have probed too freely into intimate mysteries that each of us must apprehend for himself. Allow me to say in my defense that your letters bear some responsibility for my inquiries and assertions.

My sincere thanks for the enlightenment and guidance I have received from your numerous letters. Along with your many correspondents, I have greatly profited from them.

Your affectionate brother,
Robert E. Chiles

SUGGESTIONS FOR FURTHER READING

Wesley's Journal and Letters

Curnock, Nehemiah, ed. *The Journal of John Wesley.* Standard edition, 8 vols. London: The Epworth Press, 1909-16.

Telford, John, ed. *The Letters of John Wesley.* Standard edition, 8 vols. London: The Epworth Press, 1931.

Collections from Wesley's Writings

Bewes, Richard, ed. *John Wesley's England: A 19th Century Pictorial History Based on an 18th Century Journal.* New York: Seabury, 1981.

Burtner, Robert W., and Chiles, Robert E., eds. *John Wesley's Theology: A Collection from his Works.* Nashville: Abingdon, 1982.

Curnock, Nehemiah, ed. *John Wesley's Journal.* New York: Capricorn, 1963. Abridged in one volume.

Outler, Albert C., ed. *John Wesley: A Representative Collection of his Writings.* New York: Oxford University Press, 1964.

Whaling, Frank, ed. *John and Charles Wesley: Selected Prayers, Hymns, Journal Notes, Sermons, Letters, and Treatises.* Classics of Western Spirituality. Ramsey, N.J.: Paulist Press, 1981.

About Wesley and About his Thought

Carter, Henry. *The Methodist Heritage.* New York: Abingdon-Cokesbury, 1951.

Green, Vivian H.H. *John Wesley.* London: Thomas Nelson, 1964.

Harper, Steve. *John Wesley's Message for Today.* Grand Rapids: Zondervan, 1983.

Lee, Umphrey. *The Lord's Horseman.* New York: Abingdon, 1954.

Outler, Albert C. *Evangelism in the Wesleyan Spirit.* Nashville: Tidings, 1971.

Outler, Albert C. *Theology in the Wesleyan Spirit.* Nashville: Tidings, 1975.

Snyder, Howard A. *The Radical Wesley and Patterns for Church Renewal*. Downers Grove, Illinois: Inter-Varsity, 1980.

Tuttle, Robert G. Jr. *John Wesley: His Life and Theology*. Grand Rapids: Zondervan, 1978.

Williams, Colin W. *John Wesley's Theology Today*. New York: Abingdon, 1960.

About American Methodism

McEllhenney, John G., ed. *Proclaiming Grace and Freedom: The Story of United Methodism in America*. Nashville: Abingdon, 1982.

Norwood, Frederick A. *The Story of American Methodism*. Nashville: Abingdon, 1974.

Sweet, W.W. *Methodism in American History*. Nashville: Abingdon, 1953. Revised edition.

Index

Acts, Book of, 8, 22, 31, 34, 38, 42, 54, 66, 71
Age of Reason, 112-13
Albright, Jacob, 19
Aldersgate, 19, 34, 43, 55, 57, 87-88, 109, 112
America, 14-17, 90, 91, 133
American Revolution, 14, 133
Anabaptists, 71
Antinomianism, 74, 103, 126
Apostles, 35, 42, 51, 54-55, 64, 67, 83-84, 86, 93-94, 122
Arminian Magazine, 103
Asbury, Francis, 15
Assurance, 111-13, 115-16

Baily, John, 92
Band societies, 18, 68-69, 73, 91
Baptists, 97
Bath, 61
Bell, George, 76
Bible, 26, 44, 72, 101-2, 105, 111, 116; see also Scriptures
Bigotry, 26, 39
Bradford, 36
Bribery, 133

Calling, 85-94
  based on grace, 88, 93
  time-consuming, 88-89, 97
  urgency, 88
Calvin, John, 96, 102, 125
Calvinism, 17, 44, 56, 99, 103, 104, 126-27
Camp meetings, 15
Catholic spirit, 71-72, 100-101
Catholics, 56; see also Papists
Character of a Methodist, The (Wesley), 100

Christian character, 109-11
Christian ethics, 130-33
Christian fellowship, 66-70
Christian love, 100-101, 105, 128-30
Christian perfection, 36, 75, 128-30
  gift of grace, 128-30
  realistic details, 39, 128-30
Christian tradition, 101-2, 105
Christian, Nature of, 110, 122, 127-28, 130
Christmas conference, 14
Church, Community of spirit, 66-78
  councils, 70
  New Testament, 35, 66, 70
Church of England, 18, 56, 69, 72, 97, 101-2
Church, Thomas, 99, 105, 116
Circuit riders, 15
Class meeting, 18, 68, 73, 91
Clergy. See Ministers and Preachers
Conference, 18, 73, 75, 104
Confucius, 114
Controversial correspondence, 25, 98-100
Controversy, religious, 76, 97-98, 103, 118
Conversion, miraculous, 38-40, 93, 114-16
Curnock, Nehemiah, 9, 24, 57

Deism, 56, 60, 92, 103, 114, 127
Despair, 35, 62, 118-19, 124, 128-29
Discipline, 74-78, 90, 117-18
Dissenters, 56, 69

139

Index

Divine initiative, 31-32, 40, 43, 49, 79, 113-15
Doctrine, 44, 104, 109-10, 111; see also Theology
Doctrine of Original Sin, The (Wesley), 99
Dublin, 36, 75

East Indies, 38
Edwards, Jonathan, 17
Eighteenth century England, 18, 78, 112-13, 130-33
Enthusiasm, 25, 113-17
   assurance, 115-16
   conversion, 116-17
   emotions, 76, 114-15
   miracles, 115-16, 122
   providence, 114
   work of God, 114; see also Separate Entries
Epworth, 18, 36, 46
Evangelical revival. See Wesleyan Revival
Evangelical United Brethren Church, 16
Experimental test, 38, 93, 116-17
Explanatory Notes on the New Testament (Wesley), 22, 104
Extraordinary means, 47-48, 73-74, 90-91, 131

Faith, Christian, 109-12
   gift of grace, 125, 127
   human responsibility, 125-27
   and justification, 44
   as trust, 44, 110
   and works, 122-34
Family life, 118
Fénelon, 129
Fletcher, John, 124
Foundry, 76
Free, Dr., 92
Free Methodist Church, 16

Georgia, 19, 68, 74, 87
Germany, 36
Gibson, Dr., 117
God, call of, 34, 86-94
   grace of, 35-37, 40, 44, 49; see also Grace
   initiative of, 40, 79, 113-15; see also Divine Initiative
   justice, 45
   love, 45, 79-80; see also Christian Love
   mercy, 45
   providence, 35, 37-38, 90-91, 114-15; see also Extraordinary Means
   wrath, 45
Good works, 44, 123-27, 131-33
Gospel, good news of, 45, 54
   judgment of, 61-62, 123-24
   offense of, 54-64, 91-92
   resistance to, 54-62, 91-93
Grace, 26-27, 31-32, 48-50, 124-27; see also God, Grace of
   converting, 45, 49, 124
   convincing, 45, 49, 61, 124
   falling from, 39, 67-68, 77, 126
   means of, 16, 69, 73, 103, 117, 126
   necessity, 124, 127
   prevenient, 124

Heck, Barbara, 14
Heretics, 92, 102, 104
Holiness, 69, 87, 91, 104, 109-10, 127-31; see also Christian Perfection
"Holy Club", 18, 55, 68, 87, 91
Holy Spirit and community, 66-78
   extraordinary manifestations, 48-49, 73, 90-91, 108, 113-17
   freedom in, 67, 72-74
   fruits of, 35, 38-39, 93, 112, 124, 128-30
   initiative of, 26-27, 31-32, 68-71

Index

redemptive work, 31-32, 66-68, 72-74
variation in working, 111-12
witness of, 111-12, 114-16, 118; see also Assurance
Human responsibility, 27, 79, 83-84, 89-91, 125-26, 135-36

Ignorance, 89, 98, 105
"Innovations", 17-18, 37, 73-74, 90-91, 102

Jackson, Thomas, 25
Jesus Christ, apostles of, 83
ground of salvation, 110, 124
gospel, 105
redemption, 110, 124, 126-27
John Street Church, 14
Jones, Mr., 109
Journal (Wesley), 23-25, 27, 79-80
Journal and Book of Acts, 8, 22, 25-27, 31-32, 42-43, 54-55, 66, 71
Justification by faith, 44, 46, 102, 104, 111, 125; see also Faith, Salvation

King George, 59
Knowledge, 50, 89, 104-105

Large Minutes of the Conference, 104
Law, William, 102, 103
Lay preachers, 18, 73, 90, 93
Letters (Wesley), 23, 25-27, 90, 94, 98-99, 109, 123, 130, 135-36
Letters and Paul's Letters, 8, 22, 25-27, 83-84, 86-87, 94, 96, 108-9, 122-23
Liberty of Conscience, 70-71, 133
Lincoln College, 18, 87, 99
Liquor, 133
Lloyd's Evening Post, 44
Loan fund, 131
London, 36, 56, 68, 92

Love, practice of, 98, 105, 128, 130-34
renewal through, 80, 130
resistance to, 79-80
social, 130-33
love feasts, 18
Luther, Martin, 19, 102

Mahomet, 114
Man, bondage, 61, 124-25
fallen state, 50, 57, 61, 88, 123-24
freedom, 44, 62, 125-26, 128, 130
Medical services, 131
Membership statistics, 15-17, 68, 77
Methodism, American, 14-17, 19, 73, 91
membership, 15, 17
divisions, 16
reunification, 16
Methodism, British, 14, 17-19
Methodist churches, Black, 16
Methodist doctrines, 97, 104-105
Methodist Episcopal Church, 16
Methodist Protestant Church, 16
Methodists, 34, 38, 44, 55, 70, 71, 74, 75, 76, 77, 91, 101, 112, 128, 133
Middleton, Dr. Conyers, 25, 110
Ministers, 56, 76-77, 86, 89-90; see also Preachers
Miracles, 93, 115-16; see also Extraordinary Means
Mobs, 47, 58-60, 63
Money, 132-33
Montanus, 72-73
Moore, William, 76
Moravians, 17, 56, 68, 102, 126-27
Mysticism, 103

Nelson, John, 58
New birth, 104, 124, 127-28; see also Regeneration

New England, 17, 36
New Testament, 27, 108, 110

Oglethorpe, William, 19
Old Testament, 110
Opinions, 97, 100-101, 104-5,
    109-10
Orthodoxy, 97, 101-5, 109; see
    also Doctrine
Otterbein, Philip William, 19
Oxford, 36, 63, 87, 91
Oxford University, 18, 57, 87

Papists, 56, 92
Pastoral care, 117-19
Pastoral visitation, 36, 117, 118
Pentecost, 34
Perronet, Vincent, 91, 131
Persecution, 47, 55-60, 62, 64,
    91-93
Perseverance, final, 112, 126
Politics, 133
Poverty, 132
Prayer, 73, 117
Preachers, 43-47, 58, 62-63, 76-77,
    89, 118
Preaching, authentic, 43-45, 79
    extempory, 73
    field, 18, 46-47, 56, 73, 90
    itinerant, 15, 24, 90, 118
    relevant, 45-47
    response, 50-51, 55-57, 60-62
    role, 42, 48, 49, 89, 118
    and spirit, 42-43, 47-49
Predestination, 58, 103, 126-27
Presbyterians, 71
A Preservative Against Unsettled
    Notions In Religion (Wesley),
    103
Press, attacks by, 57, 99
Prison reform, 132
Prisoners of War, 132

Quakers, 71

Reason, importance, 54, 114, 115
    limits, 98, 104-5, 115, 116
Redemptive reality, 109-19
    renewed character, 109-11
    gracious assurance, 111-13
    miraculous accompaniments,
        113-17
    pastoral confirmation, 117-19
Reformation, Protestant, 8, 101-2
Regeneration, 110, 111, 116-17,
    127-28; see also New Birth
Religion of Love, 100, 105, 110,
    122-23, 128-30, 135-36
Religious decline, 35, 38-40, 50,
    67, 75-76, 77, 91, 92-93, 97-98,
    104, 118-19
Religious liberty, 119, 128, 133
Religious transformation, 35-38,
    62-63, 93, 114-17, 127-30
Rules of The Society For the People
    Called Methodist (Wesley), 74-75

Sacraments, 56, 69, 73-74, 117
St. Agnes Church, 45
St. Bartholomew's Church, 62
St. George's Church, 14
St. Mary's Church, 57
St. Paul, 34, 54, 59, 64, 66, 83-84,
    86, 108, 122
    epistles, 8, 22, 83-84, 122
    theology, 26, 96
St. Paul's Church, 46
Salvation, final, 126, 129
    by grace, 43-45, 87,88, 124-27
    by works, 83, 87-88, 124-27;
        see also Faith, Justification
Sanctification. See Christian
    Perfection
Satanic powers, 60
Schismatics, 92
School, experimental, 131
Scriptural Christianity, 26-27, 43,
    57, 72, 90, 134

Index

Scriptures, 26, 70, 74, 101-2, 114, 116, 117, 128, 129; see also Bible
Sermons, 44, 50, 54, 99
Shadford, George, 90
Signs and wonders, 93, 108, 111, 113-16; see also Miracles
Sin, bondage, 61, 123-25
    conviction, 45, 61-62
    depravity, 123-25
    original, 61, 104, 124
    universality, 61, 124; see also Man
Slavery, 133
"Smith, John", 115-16
Smuggling, 133
Socinianism, 103
Southern Baptist Convention, 17
Stewardship, 132-33
"Stillness", 126; see Moravian
Strange's aid, 132
Strawbridge, Robert, 14

Tadcaster, 51
Taylor, John, 99
Telford, John, 8, 25, 98
Themes, basic, 7, 31-32, 79-80, 83-84, 135-36
Theology, 96-97, 101-2, 104-5, 109-10; see also Doctrine
Time, use of, 88-89, 91-97, 119
Toplady, Augustus, 99-100
Trinity, 79-80, 109
Truth, 56, 98, 101-2, 105, 108-10

United Methodist Church, 16
Universal love, 130-31; see also Catholic Spirit

War, 133
Watson, Richard, 96
Wednesbury, 59
Wesley, Charles, 18, 87, 111, 130

Wesley, John, conversion, 19, 87-88; see also Aldersgate
    courage, 59-60
    defends faith, 96-105
    defends his ministry, 93
    ecumenical spirit, 71-72, 100-101, 131
    last years, 44, 48-50, 62-64, 72, 104
    leadership, 18
    ordinations by, 73, 91
    personally attacked, 57-60, 91-93, 113-16
    pursuit of holiness, 87-88, 128
    reliance on spirit, 72-74, 91
    religious training, 18
    resisted by churches, 55-56
    seeks legal redress, 59
    summary of activity, 19, 89
    suspicious of acclaim, 63-64
    writings, 18, 22
Wesley, Samuel, 18, 112
Wesley, Samuel, Jr., 115
Wesley, Susanna, 18
Wesleyan Methodist Church, 16
Wesleyan Revival, 17-20, 26-27, 34-40, 50-51, 100, 103-4
    opposition to, 55-62, 113-17
    success of, 34, 62-64, 72, 77-78, 113, 115-17, 128
Wesleyan societies, 18, 66, 68-73, 77, 91; see also Methodists
    admission, 74-75, 100
    exclusion, 75, 91
    rules, 74-75
Wesleyan "standards", 15, 22, 104
White, John, 25
Whitefield, George, 17, 46, 102, 103, 104, 114-15
Wilberforce, William, 133
Witness of the Spirit; See Holy Spirit
Work of God, 27, 31, 34-40, 51, 90, 113-15
World parish, 71

143